THE PRELIMINARIES OF THE AMERICAN REVOLUTION AS SEEN IN THE ENGLISH PRESS 1763–1775

BY

FRED JUNKIN HINKHOUSE

1969

OCTAGON BOOKS

New York

Reprinted 1969
by special arrangement with Columbia University Press

OCTAGON BOOKS
A DIVISION OF FARRAR, STRAUS & GIROUX, INC.
19 Union Square West
New York, N. Y. 10003

AM

LIBRARY OF CONGRESS CATALOG CARD NUMBER: 70-75997

Printed in U.S.A. by
TAYLOR PUBLISHING COMPANY
DALLAS, TEXAS

KEY TO ABBREVIATIONS

C. R. The Critical Review: or, Annals of Literature.
D. A. The Daily Advertiser. (London).
Gaz. The Gazeteer and New Daily Advertiser. (London).
G. E. P. The General Evening Post. (London).
Gent. Mag. The Gentleman's Magazine and Historical Chronicle.
K. G. The Kentish Gazette. (Canterbury).
Lloyd's E. P. Lloyd's Evening Post, and British Chronicle. (London).
L. C. The London Chronicle.
London E. P. The London Evening Post.
London Mag. The London Magazine.
L. P. The London Packet.
M. J. & E. A. The Middlesex Journal and Evening Advertiser.
M. C. The Morning Chronicle, and London Advertiser.
M. P. The Morning Post, and Daily Advertiser. (London).
M. R. The Monthly Review.
P. A. The Public Advertiser. (London).
P. L. The Public Ledger. (London).
S. J. C. The St. James's Chronicle; or the British Evening Post.
        (London).
Univ. Mag. The Universal Magazine, of Knowledge and Pleasure.
W. E. P. The Whitehall Evening Post: Or, London Intelligencer.

PREFACE

THE author has endeavored to set forth in a representative manner such English opinion of the preliminaries of the American Revolution as can be seen only in the English press. For this reason letters of opinion from America or obviously from Americans as, for example, those over Franklin's signatures, and those by Arthur Lee, signed "Junius Americanus," debates in parliament, public speeches, state papers and the very voluminous pamphlet literature on the question have either been disregarded totally or touched upon only incidentally. Most of this excluded material has been worked over again and again by investigators of our revolutionary period, but little attention has been given to the sources that can be found in English newspapers and magazines alone. In the midst of material so vast in amount the author's problem has been that of choosing and sorting; but, throughout, his constant effort has been to make the presentation accurate and representative.

This, then, is by no means an attempt to write a history of the preliminaries of the American Revolution, but is rather an attempt to show how these were reflected in the English press. For this reason some knowledge of the events themselves, on the part of the reader, is taken for granted.

In this work the author is especially indebted for advice and criticism to Professors Robert Livingston Schuyler and Evarts B. Greene of Columbia University, and to the librarians of Columbia University, Yale University, the New York Public Library, the New York Historical Association Library, the British Museum, and the London Guildhall Library.   F. J. H.

7

TABLE OF CONTENTS

CHAPTER I

THE NEWSPAPERS

THE present-day reader of American newspapers, looking for expressions of opinion, turns to the editorial page. Occasionally, though at very rare intervals, he may send the editor a letter giving his own views on some subject, which may be printed under such a head as Reader's Column, Voice of the People, or What Our Readers Think. Today such letters are relatively of no consequence, as it is only occasionally that they are written by men of importance.[1] One hundred and fifty years ago in English newspapers, however, such columns and letters were very important; what is left of them today is but vestigial remains.

The reader of the English papers of the pre-Revolutionary period would have looked long for editorial points of view or "leading articles." The English printer[2] of 1763-1775 printed issue after issue, month after month of his paper, without one word of what might be called editorial matter, for editorials had not yet been developed.[3] But notwithstanding the scarcity of editorial comment, there was no dearth in expression of opinion, for every important paper of that period inserted in each issue from one to perhaps four or five letters from contributors who were generally

---

[1] These remarks are more applicable to American than to English papers.

[2] The word "editor" was little used during this period. The men in charge of the papers almost always called themselves "printers" and were so called by others.

[3] See John Wade, *Junius*, vol. ii, Preface, iii-iv (London, 1850).

volunteer and unpaid.[1] These letters gave practically the only expressions of opinion given in the papers; nor were such opinions written by nobodies, for we are told, " Influential men of all parties, " adopted " this method as the best for giving publicity to their opinions." [2] The columns of the *Public Advertiser,* says another student of English newspapers, were used by nearly every prominent man of the day.[3] These letters are a characteristic feature of English journalism in the period 1760-1775, and it is to them that the modern reader must turn if he would know what views the Englishman of that day read in his newspapers. Before 1760 the papers commonly printed essays giving current views, and soon after 1775, when leading articles began to develop, the contributed letters were forced to take the subordinate position which they have today; [4] but while they continued, they were a medium for a full and free expression of opinion such as had not existed before, and has rarely existed since.

The reason they were such a medium is to be found in the professed policy of the chief printers of the time. Since impartiality was the ideal most in repute, the great majority of papers strove for it, either in appearance or in fact. Probably the chief paper of the time was the *Public Advertiser,* conceded by all critics to have had no superiors. Fox Bourne calls it " the most influential of the daily papers published at this time." [5] Macdonagh says it was " the greatest and most successful newspaper of the period." [6] " Junius," the most famous and the most mys-

---

[1] See article on H. S. Woodfall in *Dictionary of National Biography.*

[2] Wade, *op. cit.,* Preface, iii-iv.

[3] Fox Bourne, *English Newspapers* (London, 1887), vol. i, p. 193.

[4] *Cambridge Hist. of Eng. Lit.* (Cambridge, 1907-1916), vol. ii, p.33.

[5] Fox Bourne, *op. cit.,* vol. i, pp. 181-182.

[6] Macdonagh, Michael, *The Reporter's Gallery* (London, 1913), p. 187.

terious of the letter writers of the period, chose it for his letters, which were the journalistic sensation of the day and helped materially to increase its already large circulation. Comparison with contemporary journals is highly favorable to the *Public Advertiser*. It may be said to represent the best, and it set the standard for many a lesser rival. The editorial policy of such a paper is worth knowing.

Throughout the period under review it was printed by H. S. Woodfall, the more famous of two brothers of first rank in eighteenth-century English journalism. In 1771, in a New Year's letter to his public, he told of his policy and on the subject of impartiality said, " The Public Advertiser is open to all Parties, and my Correspondents have ever been at Liberty to make it what they please. If I am discovered sometimes to be too ministerial, at others my Readers will confess I am sufficiently free with Ministers. Junius and Cinna[1] are always alike sure of Admission." [2] On another occasion, when a contributor charged him with favoring the Patriots, as the anti-Administration and pro-American party was popularly called, he wrote, " The Printer thinks it necessary to assure the Writer that his Paper is equally open to all Parties; he endeavours, with the utmost Impartiality, to arrange the Materials that are sent him, and the Public Advertiser is just what its Correspondents please to make it." [3] Again he said, " The Printer can only repeat what he has frequently declared, viz., that he endeavours to publish all the Letters he is favoured with as near in Turn as possible." [4] Still another time he declared, "The Printer looks on himself only as a purveyor. . . ." [5]

---

[1] Prominent opponent and supporter of Administration, respectively.

[2] *P. A.*, Jan. 1, 1771.

[3] *Ibid.*, March 16, 1770.

[4] *Ibid.*, Jan. 2, 1770.

[5] *Ibid.*, Sept. 2, 1769. See article on H. S. Woodfall in *D. N. B.*

Although such professions were perhaps more commonly made than practised, H. S. Woodfall remained true to them; and the reader feels that the charges of partiality infrequently made were without foundation. Both sides accused him of favoritism. "Curius Dentatus," a ministerial writer, praised him for his "impartial Conduct, which . . . caused them [the Patriots] to pronounce the Public Advertiser a ministerial Paper . . . ." [1] while "One of the Public," a critic of the ministers, wrote, "I have to return you my hearty Thanks for now and then allowing me a Place in your Paper, which I have been denied in other Papers, under various Signatures; and though I secretly accused your Delay, yet I found your Compliance at last." He then condemned those printers who were "bought off" by ministerial money to betray the people, making the not infrequent charge of the corrupting influence of the ministerial gold upon printers. [2] A well-known contemporary observer declared that Woodfall was "strictly impartial," and that ministerial and opposition letters were printed "without any other preference than priority of receipt, or than the temporary nature of the subject would demand." [3] A twentieth-century critic writes, "He was scrupulously impartial in his choice from his letter-bag. Merit and immunity from the law of libel were the only conditions exacted." [4] On American affairs the verdict must be that he lived up to his professions. Thus in 1775, up to and including August 23, the date of the king's proclamation declaring the Americans to be in rebellion, he printed 160 letters which may be classified as anti-American and 130 which may be classified as pro-

[1] *P. A.*, June 13, 1775.

[2] *P. A.*, July 22, 1775.

[3] Nichols, John, *Literary Anecdotes of the Eighteenth Century* (London, 1812), vol. i, p. 301.

[4] *Camb. Hist. of Eng. Lit.*, vol. x, p. 400.

American. Such a classification, while not exact, at least indicates that he allowed both factions to use his columns freely.

In noting the claims to impartiality put forward by Woodfall, it may be said that such expressions as those given above form a very large proportion of the material that may, in any sense, be called editorial and the few sentences here given are the gleanings from his newspaper over a period of several years. In addition to these infrequent "editorial" statements the printer's hand is shown more frequently in replies and short messages to contributors, explaining delays in printing, or giving some reason for refusal to print or for the necessity of editing.

Other papers made the same claims. William Woodfall, a younger brother, and editor of several papers in the period 1763 to 1775, published in 1776, some material that roused the wrath of David Garrick, the actor. "Hearing that Garrick had charged him with rancour, he wrote to him that 'as the printer of the Morning Chronicle I am the servant of the public—their message-carrier—their mouth-piece. . . '." [1] Again, answering a charge of partiality for the ministry brought against him by "Philalethes," he wrote, "In political matters, letters on both sides of every question have been admitted, whenever they were written with candour and correctness." [2] The files of the *Morning Chronicle,* as well as of the *London Packet,* another of his papers, show in nearly every issue that he lived up to his creed, at least as far as American affairs were concerned, for repeatedly letters and paragraphs on opposite sides of the dispute were printed on the same page. A letter-writer in the *London Chronicle,* giving the policy of a good

[1] See article on W. Woodfall in *D. N. B.* For such claims in the *P. L.,* see July 9, Aug. 14, Oct. 15, 1765, *passim.*

[2] *M. C.,* July 8, 1775.

newspaper, said "impartiality is the best recommendation, and will in the end, consequently be the surest support of a public paper." [1] "An Impartial Protestant" insinuated broadly that many papers were not what they professed to be, for he addressed a letter to the *St. James's Chronicle*, another of the leading London papers, "Trusting, Mr. Baldwin, that the St. James's Chronicle is in Reality what, perhaps, some other Papers are but in Pretence, *Open to all Parties, and influenced by none*, I depend upon your favouring this Letter with a Place in it." [2] In 1774, the *London Packet* opened a new department called the "American Budget," in which it promised to make a special effort to collect American news, and to act "with the strictest impartiality, without the least design of inflaming the minds of the public." [3] The *Kentish Gazette* made an almost identical announcement on April 13, 1774, and the *London Magazine* a similar one in August, 1774. "Junius" bore witness that the papers as a whole lived up to such claims. Addressing a letter to Doctor William Blackstone, who had recently written a pamphlet, he said:

You seem to think the Channel of a Pamphlet more respectable and better suited to the Dignity of your Cause, than that of a News-Paper. Be it so. Yet if News-Papers are scurrilous, you must confess they are impartial. They give us, without any apparent Preference, the Wit and Argument of the Ministry, as well as the abusive Dulness of the Opposition. The Scales are equally poised. It is not the Printer's Fault, if the greater Weight inclines the Balance. [4]

Though this was the prevailing policy it may not be amiss to say that exceptions were not unknown. Today a reader

[1] *L. C.*, May 17, 1764.
[2] *S. J. C.*, Aug. 25, 1767.
[3] *L. P.*, March 11, 1774.
[4] *P. A.*, July 29, and *S. J. C.*, July 29, 1769.

can classify most American papers according to their editorial position. A paper may be Republican, Democratic, Independent, Conservative or Progressive, but in every case one expects to find a consistent stand upon any given issue. Self-contradiction over any issue is so rare that when it does appear it needs much explanation. The present-day reader is likely to try to classify the mid-eighteenth-century English papers in the same way, but to do so is to fail to appreciate their journalistic policy. For nearly every issue of the leading papers printed opinion on both sides of the matter in controversy; hence it is not possible to classify the papers of 1760-1775 so precisely as those of the present day.

Next to the letters the greatest source of opinion in the papers was the paragraph. These were usually collected into columns, and loosely grouped as to subject matter. Sometimes they were pure news items, but more frequently they were news items written with a political purpose; and occasionally they were simple expressions of opinion such as today would be called editorials. The paragraphers were famous and feared in their day; sometimes a short paragraph of three or four lines caused a stir hard for us to understand. It is difficult to assign a given paragraph to a particular paper, for a pungent one was rarely allowed to appear in one journal only, but might be printed in half a dozen or more. The same is true, but to a lesser extent, of the letters. The implication is strong that shears and a pastepot were a very much used part of the printer's equipment. Sometimes the dates indicate priority for one paper and suggest that others copied from it, but often the first appearance in two or more papers was simultaneous. It is probable that copying was most frequent, but that occasionally a writer sent his paragraphs or his letters to more than one paper at the same time.[1] The reader should hesitate to

---

[1] See printer's note to correspondents, *Gaz.*, Feb. 8, 1766.

conclude that these paragraphs represented the views of the printer of the paper in which they appeared, both because of the professions of impartiality which the printers made and because the paragraphs were widely and indiscriminately printed in different papers. Since they were never signed, their value is impaired by the fact that the authorship of most of them is lost in anonymity.

The letters suffer in the same way, but sometimes it is possible to discover their authorship. The signatures given were almost always pseudonyms: " Cassius," " Cassandra," " Caesar " and " Cicero," may be found keeping company with the less pretentious " John Ploughshare," " Timothy Hint," " Homespun " and " A Cobbler." Among the endless variety of signatures the classical were strong favorites. In identifying writers of the letters internal evidence gives few trustworthy clues, but the pseudonyms themselves sometimes do.[1] These, however, cannot be trusted too implicitly, for there being no copyright on them a writer might inadvertently or even wilfully use a signature that had been used already by somebody else. H. S. Woodfall rebuked a contributor thus: " The Writer of the Letter signed M. R. could not surely imagine the Printer of this Paper would aid in an attempt to impose on the Public by publishing a Letter under the Signature of Junius, which he must know is not the Production of that Writer ";[2] and more frequently he changed a signature or asked that one be changed when new writers used signatures which were " in some Measure, the Property of his old Friends."[3] In addition, " the same author would vary his pseudonyms as much as possible, chiefly with intent to avoid discovery and the decrease of credit which his communications might undergo if

[1] See appendix for pseudonyms that have been identified.
[2] P. A., Jan. 21, 1775.
[3] P. A., March 21, 1770.

he were known, but also, to provide sham opponents as a
foil to his arguments and to create an illusion of wide public
support for his views." [1]   Notice has been taken of a writer
who sought to have his letters accepted by unfriendly printers through changing his signatures.[2]   Benjamin Franklin,
who was in England during a large part of the pre-revolutionary period, was given to using various signatures in his
frequent contributions to the papers.   Smyth, in Franklin's
collected *Writings,* gives letters with the following signatures: "A Traveller," "Pacificus Secundus," "Homespun,"
" F. B.," " B. F.," " F-S, " " New-England," " Medius,"
" N. M. C. N. P. C. H.," " Francis Lynn, *of Boston in
New England,*" " A new Englandman," " A New England
Man," "A well-wisher to the King and all His Dominions,"
" N. N.," " A. P.," " A Londoner," " B. Franklin," and
" A Friend to the Poor."   It is probable that this list of
eighteen signatures does not contain all that Franklin used.
" Junius " also was credited with many pseudonyms.   The
signatures seldom give clues which lead to the identification
of the writers.   Any person who takes the trouble to investigate the efforts made to identify the author of the letters
of "Junius," the most famous anonymous letters of the time,
and perhaps of all time, will speedily learn some of the difficulties attendant upon such efforts.[3]   William Cushing, in
*Initials and Pseudonyms: a Dictionary of Literary Dis-
guises,* identifies a few, others have been discovered in a
fortuitous manner, but for the most part the identity of the
writers is lost, apparently beyond recall.

---

[1] *Cambridge Hist. of Eng. Lit.,* vol. x, pp. 400-401.

[2] *Cf. supra,* p. 14.

[3] " A Manuscript bibliography of Junius, edited by Robert F. Pick, in
the Vassar College Library, lists one hundred and fifty-nine different
editions of Junius, one hundred and forty-three titles of works relative
to the subject, and sixty-two names of persons for whom the authorship
of the letters has been claimed." Salmon, L. M., *The Newspaper and
the Historian* (New York, 1923), p. 422 n.

While the names of these writers would add value to a study that must pay major attention to the letters, yet the lack of them by no means deprives the letters of all value. If we cannot determine who held such opinions, we can at least know that such opinions were held, and, if a number of apparently unconnected writers expressed similar sentiments, we may conclude that those sentiments were common in the period. The simple fact that certain ideas and viewpoints were printed in the English papers is also of value, for we are thus able to learn what the newspaper-reading English public knew about the dispute. The fact that so large an amount of the opinion printed in the English papers is favorable to the American cause, is also not without great significance. Regardless of all the propagandist efforts the Americans may have brought to bear, it is highly improbable that English printers would have inserted so much material favorable to the colonies unless there had been in England a large and influential section of the population that looked upon the measures of the administration with disfavor.

In attempting to evaluate the material found, several allowances must be kept in mind; otherwise serious errors may be made. First, one can rarely be sure of the source of the opinion, and therefore, while apparently reading what some Englishman thought of the American issues, one may be reading what some American in England wrote for the good of the cause. Franklin was in England during the years when the revolution was brewing, and, as we have seen, he was actively writing for the papers. As his collected writings show, he frequently sent news and letters to the papers with the purpose of influencing public opinion. In a letter written to Charles Thompson during the Stamp Act troubles, he said, " I have reprinted everything from America, that I thought might help our Common Cause." [1] Arthur

[1] *Writings,* Smyth ed., vol. iv, p. 411; see vol. iv, p. 463, vol. v, pp. 42, 75, 90, 91, 252.

Lee was another American who pursued the same tactics. In a letter of September 18, 1769, he wrote, " I have laboured much to make the cause of America popular, in which if I have been assisted [*sic*] by the American agents, I have not the least doubt of having succeeded." [1]   His signature was "Junius Americanus," a pseudonym he strove to make popular with the English, writing to his brother that in his efforts to make it so he did not confine the series to purely colonial affairs, for " to make what was written *in defence of the colonies acceptable,* it was necessary, now and then, to aim a stroke at characters *obnoxious here*." [2]   That other Americans were doing the same sort of thing is certain, but for the most part it seems impossible to discover their letters.   When such letters have been identified in this study they have been disregarded.

Complaints of propaganda were not uncommon.   Thus when some shipwrights went on strike in July, 1775, a paragraph reported that the troubles "prove to have been fomented by some American Agents here, who are very busy in rendering themselves as useful as possible to the rebels, their masters. . . ." [3]   Other paragraphs stated that American advocates were very busy in London, but that their conduct would " rather injure than strengthen the cause of their employers," [4] and that a certain letter purporting to have been written in Boston " like many others was originally written by an American here." [5]   "A State Tinker," a prominent anti-American writer in the *Public Advertiser,* declared that " Dr. Quinancy [Quincy], and a near Relation of the notorious Electrical Doctor [Franklin], are at present upon

[1] R. H. Lee, *Life of Arthur Lee* (Boston, 1829), vol. i, p. 191 ; see p. 190.

[2] *Ibid.,* p. 19 ; see p. 197.

[3] *L. P.,* July 5, 1775.

[4] *L. P.,* April 1, 1774.

[5] *L. C.,* Dec. 3, 1774.

a Tour through England along with other Emissaries of the same Kidney. Their Business is to kindle the Sparks of Sedition where they are not already lighted, and where they are to blow up the Fire and supply it with Fuel." [1]   A common charge in January, 1775, when American sympathizers were petitioning for them, was that these petitions were the direct result of propagandist efforts put forward by the Americans.[2]   One may be certain, then, that Americans often masqueraded as Englishmen, and equally certain that one is not always able to penetrate the disguise, and may be deceived by such subterfuges just as contemporary Englishmen must have been.

The propaganda, however, was not all on one side. The administration often felt the need of public support and sought to gain it or to create its appearance in the papers. It is entirely probable that they secured the insertion of more material in the papers than did the Americans and their friends, for they had a large treasury and no hesitancy as to using it. Hence the investigator has the difficulty of weighing letters written by Americans, and letters written by the administration or inspired by administration gold, besides those written by Englishmen with no axes to grind.

The opposition did not fail to denounce ministerial methods. A paragrapher, showing the almost universal anti-Scotch animus, combined with a love of America, declared, " Two long well known Caledonian authors, . . . are employed at the rate of a guinea a column for writing against America and the people, who pay amazing sums for the insertion of their poisonous draughts." [3]   It was asserted that Lord N——h actually spent " much more than the amount

[1] *P. A.*, Feb. 28, 1775 and March 9, 1775.

[2] *L. C.*, Jan. 21, 31, 1775; see *M. J. & E. A.*, Nov. 29, 1774 and *P. A.*, Feb. 18, 1775.

[3] *L. P.*, July 26, 1775; see *K. G.*, Aug. 16, 1775.

of the salaries of his different offices in maintaining a parcel of worthless, mercenary scribblers." [1]   "A Liveryman," charged, with plausible detail, that a number of anti-American letters were printed for pay.[2]   Another writer spoke of " The host of pitiful Scribblers . . . retained in constant pay, for the purpose of misrepresenting and slandering the Americans. . . ." [3]   The printer of *Lloyd's Evening Post,* below a letter signed " Creon," wrote, " **** The letters written with this signature deserve attention, as they . . . seem to be the production of a Gentleman well acquainted with the intention of Government; and written as a prelude to feel the pulse of the Public." [4]

It is certain, then, that both sides used propaganda and it is probable that the administration profited by it more than the opposition.   Remembering the journalistic policy of impartiality, one understands why the papers were very much on the order of a debating rostrum or, as H. S. Woodfall, speaking of his own paper, put it, like a " Cockpit for Political Spurring," [5] where each could speak his mind freely. Although some papers may have discriminated, it is certain that in the English press as a whole the Americans and their friends had no difficulty in getting their side presented, and indeed, contemporary complaint of discrimination was practically non-existent.   That contemporaries did not always know just where a paper stood is indicated by a letter which Franklin wrote to his son in reference to one he had written for the *London Chronicle,* which by some has been called a

[1] *L. P.,* Aug. 11, 14, 1775.

[2] *P. A.,* Feb. 11, 1768; see Feb. 4, 1775.

[3] *L. C.,* Dec. 29, 1774.

[4] *Lloyd's E. P.,* May 11, 1770. This letter signed " Messala " was printed in the *P. A.,* Feb. 20, 1775.

[5] *P. A.,* Jan. 1, 1766.

Tory paper.[1] The letter, Franklin said, had been changed until it could neither " scratch nor bite," but seemed only " to paw and mumble." His comment was, " The editor of that paper, one Jones, seems a Grenvillian, or is very cautious, as you will see by his corrections." [2] Contributors to the press frequently charged that, though the English papers were impartial and printed much on the American side, there was not a " single news-paper on the entire continent of British America, which would admit so much as a paragraph in favour of the Mother Country." [3] This charge was, however, without justification.

Again, in evaluating this material, the reader must allow for the partisan politics of the day. In doing this some knowledge of present-day politics should prove valuable. Increasingly as the years went by from 1765 to 1775 the American question became partisan, so that in the latter part of the period the lines of faction were closely drawn. In the last few years those in favor of the administration were anti-American as a matter of course, while all who opposed the administration seized upon the American issue as one likely to be embarrassing, and accordingly played it up. Neither side could claim that its arguments always had the ring of sincerity, and the conviction is borne home that the anti-administration, pro-American factions most often lacked that admirable quality. They were the " outs," and any issue with which they could belabor the " ins " would serve.

The reader must also make allowance for the great increase in the size of newspapers since 1770. The modern reader, at least if he is American, is accustomed to huge

[1] It is so classified by Marks, *England and America 1763-83* (London, 1907), vol. i, p. 34, and by Fox Bourne, *op. cit.*, vol. i, p. 197.

[2] *Writings*, Smyth ed., vol. v, p. 90.

[3] See *L. P.*, May 9, 1774. *M. C.*, Dec. 14, 1774. *P. A.*, May 30, 1774.

headlines and column after column devoted to events of comparative insignificance. But in those days huge headlines had not been thought of and rarely did an article get even a heading. An article that occupied as much space as two or three modern columns was so exceptional as commonly to call forth some explanation on the part of the writer or printer, in excuse of its length. Instead of a page, an important report received a column; perhaps only a paragraph. The reader is likely to be deceived by the space allotments. Unconsciously measuring by modern journalistic standards, he tends to impute insignificance to any article without headlines and without great length. A paragraph of half a dozen lines with no heading is easily passed over, but often such a report comprised all that was vouchsafed to the reader for an event that today would be given columns or even special editions.

The reason for this difference is clear. Modern papers, as products of an industrial civilization, are turned out with a speed and a cheapness impossible to an earlier age.[1] The industrial revolution has revolutionized the press, and the consequent change in size is the first to make an impression on the present-day reader. The most popular size of the earlier day was eleven and a half by eighteen and a quarter inches, only half the size of our modern American journals. Four such pages made a complete issue. Just what this means may be realized when, on comparison one sees that one forty-eight-page issue of the New York *Times* carries as much printed matter as twenty-four *Public Advertisers* of 1775, or as much as the *Public Advertiser* would print in a month, for there were no Sunday editions. Six such daily numbers of the New York *Times* and one Sunday edition would be more than two-thirds the size of a daily paper

---

[1] The steam engine was first applied to a newspaper press in 1814.

of 1775 for a year. Two ordinary weeks of the New York *Times* would more than equal a year of the English paper.

Another important difference is in price. Two cents is a common price to pay today, while two pence half-penny [five cents] was the standard newspaper price in 1775 for a newspaper which contained about one-twentieth of the reading matter of a modern metropolitan journal. If we take into account the decrease in the purchasing power of money since 1770 the difference is still greater. The cause, of course, is the industrial revolution. The slow hand press did the printing then; now huge power presses turn off thousands of papers per hour. Type was then set by hand; it is now set by machinery. The paper used was expensive rag paper. Now cheap wood-pulp paper goes into our journals. As transportation was slow and difficult, papers had a more restricted area of circulation. The slowness of communications also greatly hindered the newspapers in gathering news. A fast ship, sent to America about the middle of November, could not be expected back, said a paragraph, until the latter end of March.[1] The reading public was much smaller, not only because of the higher price of the papers, but also because the proportion of illiteracy was much greater then than it is now. "Will Alfred" was speaking truly when he wrote, "the common People don't purchase Newspapers."[2] Advertising, now the chief economic support of journalism, was known then, but it had not been developed to anything like its present extent. Newspapers even paid theaters for theatrical notices.[3]

The figures of circulation seem small to us. The *Gentleman's Magazine* was perhaps the chief monthly publication

[1] *P. A.*, Nov. 15, 1768.

[2] *P. A.*, Oct. 22, 1765.

[3] Fox Bourne, *op. cit.*, vol. i, p. 196; Grant, *The Newspaper Press* (London, 1871), vol. i, p. 202.

of the time. " Johnson says its (circulation) was over ten
thousand in 1739. . . . A few years later it had risen to
fifteen thousand." Figures are most easily available for the
Public Advertiser, but they sometimes contradict each other.
Nichols says that the letters of Dr. James Scott, written in
1765 and signed " Anti-Sejanus " " were so popular that
they raised the sale of the paper from 1,500 to 3,000 a
day." [1] According to Fox Bourne, its circulation in January, 1765, before "Junius" began to write for it, was less
than two thousand a day. While "Junius" was writing, it
became a little over three thousand.[2] Fox Bourne's estimate
based upon some figures in *The Athenæum* seems to be the
most reliable.[3] Grant, however, says he believes "Dr. Johnson was much nearer the truth when he expressed his belief
that from six to seven thousand was the number printed." [4]
He takes note of estimates as high as twenty thousand and
as low as three thousand five hundred, but rejects both ex-
tremes. *The Whisperer,* an ephemeral paper first published
February 17, 1770, which gave great prominence to
American sentiment, was contemporaneously reported to
have sold 12,000 of the first thirteen numbers and 187,795
of the first fifty-seven. This circulation was so large that
it caused much comment.[5] Probably few papers, if any, sur-
passed the *Public Advertiser.*

It must not be supposed that political opinion had to depend upon newspapers only for circulation, for in that day
the newspaper was still subordinate, for political purposes,

[1] Nichols, *Lit. Anecdotes of the 18th Cen.* (London, 1812), vol. ix, p. 725.

[2] Fox Bourne, *op. cit.,* vol. i, p. 195; Fox Bourne writes *Daily Advertiser*
instead of *Public Advertiser,* the context clearly showing he has made a
mistake.

[3] *Athenaeum,* July, 1848, July, 1849; nos. 1082, 1083, 1132.

[4] Grant, *op. cit.,* vol. i, p. 195.

[5] *Lloyd's E. P.,* May 14, 1770; *M. J. & E. A.,* March 21, 1771; see *P. A.,*
March 7, 1770, and Nichols, *op. cit.,* vol. iv, p. 97.

to the pamphlet.[1] The more important pamphlets were always noticed in the *Monthly Review* and the *Critical Review,* and the newspapers and the magazines, especially the latter, commonly gave large extracts from them. Prominent pamphlets, such as Johnson's *Taxation No Tyranny* for example, always caused great discussions in the papers. Not infrequently newspaper letters were afterwards collected and issued as pamphlets as was the case with Cartwright's *American Independence the Interest and Glory of Great Britain,* Thomas Crowley's *Letters and Dissertations on Various Subjects,* and Allan Ramsay Jr.'s *Letters on the Present Disturbance in Great Britain and Her American Provinces.*

Though in most ways the press was less free then than now, advantage occasionally lies with the press of 1775. The greatest restriction put upon the papers was in the reporting of parliamentary debates or anything relating to parliamentary proceedings. So rigidly enforced were the rules of parliamentary secrecy that papers were occasionally fined, simply for naming a member of the House of Lords, no matter if the mention were in an article of no political significance whatever, and regardless of whether the Lord named cared or not.[2] Parliamentary reports were not surposed to be given at all during the early part of the period under review, but the papers paid little heed to the ban and published what they could get of the proceedings. Their reports were obtained under difficulties, were likely at any time to involve them in prosecutions, and left much to be desired from the standpoint of fullness and accuracy. The chief restrictions that the papers observed were that names were commonly indicated by the first and last letters as P—t for Pitt, B—ke for Burke, etc., and that the reports were

[1] Tyler, *Lit. Hist. of the Am. Revolution,* vol. i, p. 18.
[2] Grant, *op. cit.,* vol. i, p. 172; Andrews, *op. cit.,* vol. i, pp. 196-197.

not printed for several months after the debates had taken place; for example, debates that took place over the Stamp Act in December and January were not printed until the following September.

In the history of the freedom of the English press, no period is more important than that embraced by the years 1763-1775. More was done during those years to liberate it than during any other period in English history. This is not the place to consider the famous conflicts associated with the name of John Wilkes and with his paper, the *North Briton*, which ushered in the period, nor the great struggle of 1771, which in practice, if not in theory, gave the papers the right, which they have had ever since, to print parliamentary debates.[1] While they were henceforth unmolested by serious restrictions as to printing, they certainly were not free from apprehensions of interference.

Although the papers as early as 1763 occasionally flouted the restrictions on printing and openly headed their reports " Parliamentary Proceedings," even in 1775 it was not uncommon for them to be given such disguised headings as " Debates of a Political Club," " Debates of a Political Society " or " Proceedings in a Great Political Assembly." In 1771 the *London Magazine* printed " Debates of a Political Club," and during most of the year, instead of giving the first and last letters of the speaker's names, it used appropriate Roman or Romanized names and the reader learned that " Victor Americanus replied to Horatius Tullius and was supported by Sulpicius Strado (Lord C—m.)," or that " Caius Tarquinius (the D. of G.) spoke next in the debate." This was during the last great parliamentary

[1] These struggles can be followed in Grant, Fox Bourne, Macdonagh, Andrews, Pebody, *op. cit.;* in Porritt, *Unreformed House of Commons* (Cambridge, 1903), vol. i, p. 595 *et seq.,* and in May, *The Constitutional Hist. of Eng.* (London, 1912), vol. i, chap. vii.

attempt to prevent the printing of the debates. From the latter part of 1771 the *London Magazine* printed the names of the speakers with no disguises. After 1771 the reports of the debates were fuller, though still very incomplete, and were printed soon after they had taken place, other publications besides the *London Magazine* which was typical, taking advantage of the victory to " adopt a new plan " in regard to them.[1]

This freedom of the press, such as it was, was highly prized, and every attempt to curtail it brought forth numerous protesting letters and paragraphs. The various prosecutions instituted against editors in this period were not well reported, but freedom of the press in the abstract was a common theme.[2] "Gracchus" said that all allowed it to be " the great palladium of our constitution," for when encroachments were made on liberty, the press sounded " the alarm from one end of the island to the other." [3] In similar phrase, "A Captain in the Navy" declared it to be the most important of all the " national Advantages which Great Britain enjoys over her Neighbours." [4] It was reported that a favorite toast was, " Detested shall be the man who shall form a scheme for abridging the liberty of the press and forever detested be the Minister who shall patronize it." [5] Letters about the press were common in 1763 and early in 1764 when the *North Briton* case was uppermost, and in 1770 and 1771, when the last great attempt was made to prevent the printing of the debates; but the period when the papers showed the greatest anxiety lest their freedom be taken away, was in 1774. A number of printers were in

---

[1] *London Mag.*, preface to bound volume for 1771.

[2] *Gaz.*, Feb. 4, 16, 1767.

[3] *L. P.*, Jan. 13, 1772; see *Whisperer*, Aug. 11, 25, 1770.

[4] *P. A.*, Nov. 20, 1771.

[5] *L. P.*, Jan. 24, 1774.

difficulty in that year, chief among whom were the Woodfall
brothers and J. Miller. The latter was confined in the Fleet
Street prison, from which he wrote a number of letters on
his case. The paragraphers were especially bitter during
this period against the " Cub," as Charles James Fox was
called, and in dozens of paragraphs denounced him for his
vigorous attempts to destroy the liberties of the press.[1] His
dissolute life laid him open to criticism, and advantage was
taken of his every weakness.

The precariousness of a printer's life may be judged from
the experiences of H. S. Woodfall, whose punishments for
political offenses " formed, he said, a kind of anti-climax of
retribution." He explained that " he had been *fined* by the
House of Lords; *confined* by the House of Commons; *fined
and confined* by the Court of King's Bench; and *indicted* at
the Old Baily." [2]

Although the papers were much fettered in reporting
parliamentary proceedings, apparently they were little hindered in printing opinion concerning American affairs; and
even after hostilities had begun they showed few traces of
such repression. For a time, it appears, news was cut off
at the source, but the papers printed what they could get.
It is doubtful if any present-day government would permit
papers to print so much in favor of its enemies as did the
English papers after Lexington and Bunker Hill.

In November, 1774, attempts at the censorship of news
were first denounced in the papers. It was reported that all
news from America would have to come to the papers in-
directly from France, Spain or Holland, as the ministry had
put plans into effect " to prevent them receiving it the other
way." [3] The plans of the government do not appear to

---

[1] *L. P.,* March 2, 4, 9, 23, Feb. 18, 21, 1774 *passim;* the other papers
were much the same.

[2] Nichols, *op. cit.,* vol. i, p. 301.

[3] *L. P.,* Nov. 7, 1774.

have been very successful. Rumors from America were rife, said another paragraph, but could not be verified " as the American papers are industriously kept from the London printers, by the agents of the post-office." [1] Other items of the same kind were not infrequent during this period.[2]

The evidence indicates that the printers had a high and noble conception of their office. This is revealed especially in the letters defending the freedom of the press. Early in the period " Watchman " wrote of the printer that, " In a free country he is one of the first servants of the Publick, and one of the best bulwarks of freedom, if his sentiments and abilities be correspondent with the dignity of his station. . . . The character of a Printer ought to be as upright and as unspotted as that of a Priest." [3] In the preface to the *London Magazine* for 1771 the editor wrote, " Magazines, if well conducted, will always prove barometers of the times, and show how the spirit of politics, of religion, of gallantry, and of other pursuits, rises or sinks." [4]

The magazines that have been examined carefully in this study are the *Gentleman's Magazine, Town and Country Magazine, London Magazine, Universial Magazine, Critical Review* and *Monthly Review.* The last two reviewed the books and pamphlets of the time and are valuable to any one wishing a knowledge of the pamphlet material. The *Gentleman's Magazine* was the oldest of these publications, as well as one of the best, and the others were modeled after it, more or less closely. They printed many letters, some contributed but many, perhaps most, culled from the newspapers, to which they were more closely related in subject

[1] *L. P.,* Nov. 4, 1774.

[2] See *L. P.,* Nov. 7, Dec. 23, 1774; *M. J. & E. A.,* Nov. 3, 29, 1774; *K. G.,* Nov. 9, 1774; *M. C.,* Nov. 3, 1774; *P. A.,* Jan. 11, 1775.

[3] *L. C.,* May 17, 1764.

[4] *Lond. Mag.,* preface to volume for 1771.

matter than are modern monthlies. Besides letters, the magazines contained some news, poetry, historical chronicles, lists of deaths, scientific discussions and the like. They were much less specialized than modern magazines, as may be seen from the following title page of the *Universal Magazine:*

The Universal Magazine of Knowledge and Pleasure: Containing News, Letters, Debates, Poetry, Musick, Biography, History, Geography, Voyages, Criticism, Translations, Philosophy, Mathematicks, Husbandry, Gardening, Cookery, Chemistry, Mechanicks, Trade, Navigation, Architecture and other Arts and Sciences Which may render it Instructive and Entertaining to Gentry, Merchants, Farmers and Tradesmen. To which occasionally will be added An Impartial Account of Books in several Langauges and the State of Learning in Europe; Also of the Stage, New Operas, Plays and Oratorios.

Other magazines likewise strove to be "universal."

Like the newspapers, the magazines as a rule observed neutrality on the American disputes, but they revealed their bias a little more clearly than did the papers. Of these monthly publications, the *London Magazine* and the *Monthly Review* were friendly to the Americans. The *Critical Review* was decidedly hostile. The attitude of the two reviews is revealed chiefly by the fact that the *Critical Review* almost invariably attacked pro-American pamphlets severely while the *Monthly Review* was friendly to them. This can be seen, for example, in the reviews given to two pamphlets by Otis, *The Rights of the British Colonies Asserted and Proved,* and *Considerations on Behalf of the Colonists. In a letter to a noble Lord.*[1] The attitude of the *London Mag-*

[1] The first in *M. R.,* April, 1765, p. 151 and in *C. R.,* Nov., 1764, p. 396; the second in *M. R.,* Nov., 1765, p. 399 and in *C. R.,* Oct., 1765, pp. 313-314; see a characterization of the two reviews, *Mass. Hist. Soc. Collections,* vol. 74, p. 112; see *Gaz.,* Sept. 10, 1767.

zine is shown largely in the same way and also by occasional pro-American statements that appear to be editorial.[1]   The other magazines took no decided stand but seemed inclined toward the American side.   Except in the case of the *Critical Review*, complete files of the magazines mentioned have been consulted.

The newspapers that have been examined are the *London Chronicle, St. James's Chronicle, Public Advertiser, London Packet, Lloyd's Evening Post, Gazetteer and New Daily Advertiser, Middlesex Journal and Evening Advertiser, Middlesex Journal and Chronicle of Liberty* (which in June, 1772, changed its name to the *Middlesex Journal and Universal Evening Post*), *General Evening Post, London Evening Post, Morning Chronicle, Public Ledger* and the *Whisperer,* all of London, *Adam's Weekly Courant* (Chester), *Kentish Gazette, British Chronicle, or Pugh's Hereford Journal, Chester Chronicle, Gloucester Journal, Ipswich Journal, Jackson's Oxford Journal, Newcastle Chronicle* and the *Newcastle Journal.*   For several of the London papers, practically complete files have been examined but in no case has a complete file of any provincial paper been consulted.   No paper has been included in the above list, whether London or provincial, unless complete files of a solid month or more have been surveyed in one of the periods when American affairs were especially prominent, as for example, the Stamp Act period, or in 1774 and 1775.   For most of the papers listed complete files of several years have been consulted.

Files of the provincial papers are scarce and those covering complete years in this period are very rare.   Use has been made of those in the British Museum but no attempt

---

[1] See reviews July, 1774, p. 343; Aug., 1775, p. 428; and appendix, 1774, pp. 641-648, where twelve publications dealing with American affairs are reviewed.

has been made to examine the more complete files in various local libraries. The examination that has been made of the provincial papers shows that they had little originality, and the author agrees with Fox Bourne, when he says of the press before 1829, that there is little need to examine the provincial newspapers " as, till recently, the provincial press has been to a large extent a reflex and imitation of the London press." [1] They generally had little local news, and the comment on colonial affairs was taken almost entirely from London papers or London news letters and did not differ from that in the metropolitan press. [2]

[1] Fox Bourne, *op. cit.*, vol. i, p. 379.

[2] Two interesting books on the provincial press are Austin Roland, *Robert Raikes the Elder, and the ' Gloucester Journal';* and a *History of the Northampton Mercury;* see bibliography.

CHAPTER II

Before the Stamp Act

In the years before the French and Indian War began to loom up, the English newspapers and magazines showed little interest in America, and accordingly their readers were ill-informed of colonial conditions. West Indian affairs, especially those of Jamaica, and the troubles of the English traders with the Spaniards, were featured in the little news that was printed. When the trouble with the French began to point toward a war, much more information was given, and though the increasing interest seems to have been caused by the prospect of hostilities, it was general in nature, dealing with the climate, products, people and general value of the colonies.

The dearth of news from America prior to the French and Indian War apparently does not indicate that the English had no knowledge or appreciation of the value of the colonies. If one assumes the opposite he will have to suppose that the intelligent interest shown immediately after the troubles began, was the result of knowledge gained during a few short months. The scarcity of news from America prior to 1755 is to be interpreted in the light of the maxim, " No news is good news." Even in the lulls in the colonial controversies between 1763 and 1775 the English press exemplified the adage by printing little. Before the war the news from America most worth publishing was that which foreshadowed that contest.

In the years before the Stamp Act controversy, journalistic reports from America showed fewer anticipations of trouble and less interest in America than at any other time of the pre-revolutionary era. The English reader learned of many Indian troubles in America, and, in the same reports, much about Indian customs, especially those of warfare. He read various accounts of the new territories that had come to England as a result of the French and Indian War, and, if interested, he gained a respectable knowledge of them. Toward the latter part of the period, occasional letters and paragraphs told him that Americans objected to the Sugar Act; he was informed that there was a shortage of currency in the colonies; and in reading of American manufacturing ventures, if he had been observant, he saw that many Englishmen took a keen interest in them because they thought that the development of manufactures in America would be a hard blow to England. He perhaps learned that some believed that the proprietary provinces were much more given to unrest and confusion than the crown colonies, and that a few thought the proprietary colonies should all be made into the latter.[1] Thus the well-informed reader knew that all was not well in America, but he could scarcely have realized that a serious situation was brewing.

Information concerning the American Indians was greater in volume than any other news coming from across the Atlantic. One great cause for this was the Conspiracy of Pontiac, about which a great deal of news was printed. Detached outrages also received much attention and there were frequent letters and articles descriptive of Indian habits. The Cherokees were the Indian tribe most frequently mentioned.

---

[1] *L. C.*, Nov. 10, 1764; *Lloyd's E. P.* and *P. L.*, Aug. 14, 1765 had paragraphs stating divers appeals had come from America asking that the proprietary colonies be annexed to the crown.

The reader was often led to suspect that the French were conspiring with the Indians against English interests. Prominent in connection with Indian news were the names of Sir William Johnson and Major Robert Rogers, two famous agents. The *Gentleman's Magazine* printed a six-page report of the Conestogoe Indian massacre in Lancaster County, Pennsylvania, a report especially recommended because it was said to have been written by Benjamin Franklin.[1] The massacre was reported in other magazines as well. The same magazine also gave, "An impartial account of the rise and proceedings of the Paxton Volunteers in Pennsylvania, &c." [2]

The Indian situation was recognized as serious and the need of a solution was clearly felt. An opinion of the cause of the Indian unrest was expressed in a letter from America. It was said to have been " first occasioned, as per general Opinion, by settleing on some Lands without making regular Purchases from the Indians, and not evacuating the Western Forts, or buying those Lands of them at the Conclusion of the French War." [3]   Peter Collinson, Esq., F. R. S., in two proposals for settling the difficulties, expressed the same opinion [4] and a correspondent was moved to examine the rights the Indians had to the lands in America, concluding they had a right to only as much as they used.[5] Thus Englishmen who followed American news were prepared for the Royal Proclamation of October 7, 1763, which, as an attempted solution, for purposes of settlement,

[1] *Gent. Mag.*, April, 1764, pp. 173-178.

[2] *Gent. Mag.*, June, 1764, pp. 263-265.

[3] *S. J. C.*, July 28, 1764.

[4] *Gent. Mag.*, Sept., 1763.

[5] *L. C.*, Oct. 27, 1763; see proclamation by James Hamilton, issued in June, 1763, in *Lloyd's E. P.*, July 29, 1763, and a letter by " Americanus " in the same issue.

definitely placed control of all Indian lands and recently acquired territories in the Crown. The proclamation was widely printed. A letter by "Americanus" contained a condemnation of the policy, which he thought the government had in mind, of reserving permanently all lands west of the mountains for the savages, but this was an isolated complaint, and in general the newly announced policy caused no adverse comment.[1]

The publicity given to this proclamation shows interest in the newly acquired possessions. Though the majority of Englishmen were probably indifferent to these acquisitions,[2] some were gifted with prophetic vision, and hence the printers thought a little mention of the new lands appropriate. There were a few echoes of the partisan conflict over the peace with the French in 1763, in which it had been sharply debated whether Canada should not be restored in lieu of some of the French West India islands. To some the retention of Canada seemed a poor bargain when rich sugar islands might have been had,[3] for it should be remembered that at this time many Englishmen considered their West India islands of more value than the continental colonies.[4]

In 1763 the *Gentleman's Magazine* printed several articles on the western country, the first being on, "Louisiana, or the Western Parts of Virginia and Carolina, and of the Countries that lie on both sides of the Mississippi," which gave a large two-page map of the region and much advice to prospective settlers.[5] "Candidus" described the natural products of the region in a highly optimistic report. "May

[1] *S. J. C.*, Jan. 10, 1764.

[2] See Alvord, *Mississippi Valley in British Politics* (Cleveland, 1917), vol. i, p. 84.

[3] *S. J. C.*, Sept. 24, 1763; *Gent. Mag.*, Oct., 1763, p. 496; *Lloyd's E. P.*, Aug. 8, Sept. 7, 26, 1763.

[4] *Infra*, p. 45n.

[5] *Gent. Mag.*, June, Aug., Oct., 1763.

we not ask," he wrote, "when this country is improved, what nation in the world can parallel these? what kingdom furnish such a list, . . . if these things are so what nation can equal our colonies? or what kingdom or people rival them in the articles of universal commerce?"[1]   The territory in general was looked upon as a land of promise and of future value to England but as one very much in need of settlers.   Reports of new colonies to be established in Louisiana appeared during the year 1763.   A colony was to be founded upon "the finest part of the Ohio" and called New Wales in honor of the prince.[2]   American lands were to be granted to ex-soldiers with the double purpose of giving them employment and of settling and improving the American conquests.[3]   In March, 1763, the *Universal Magazine* printed a large map of America and gave its readers a list of fourteen other maps which it had printed during the last few years.   After the royal proclamation of October, 1763, however, the notices of colonization schemes became less frequent.

Florida came in for much comment and divergent descriptions.   The *Universal Magazine* thought it a "proper subject for present Animadversion" because it was "an Acquisition likely to become of much future Use and Consideration to us,"[4] and *Lloyd's Evening Post* thought that a letter written about it in 1754 by Thomas Robinson, could not "but be acceptable to our readers."[5]   An article in the *Gentleman's Magazine* carefully described its soil and Indians and supplied its readers with a two-page map.[6]   Other

[1] *L. C.*, Jan. 6, 1763.
[2] *L. C.*, June 11, 18, 1763.
[3] *L. C.*, Sept. 13 and *S. J. C.*, Sept. 13, 1763; see *L. C.*, Nov. 3, 1763.
[4] *Univ. Mag.*, Sept., 1763.
[5] *Lloyd's E. P.*, Aug. 29, 1763.
[6] *Gent. Mag.*, Oct., 1763.

publications did the same, so that the reader could easily learn something of this newly acquired land.

How to evaluate what he might read was another matter. Perhaps some present-day Florida real-estate dealers have simply taken lessons from a few of the earliest English settlers. Some of the accounts were rosy and spoke of its "prodigious fine Climate" and of its soil, fertile even though sandy.[1] There were travelers to whom it appeared a terrestrial paradise. But other observers were more critical. A writer from St. Augustine said, "Believe me, the English papers have greatly exaggerated in their favourable accounts of this place. I never saw in my life a more unpromising spot, though I have been a sojourner in both the Indies."[2] Another letter declared that it was not a "terrestrial paradise" but "the most sandy, barren, and desert land that eyes could see, or imagination paint!"[3] A gentleman, writing from Pensacola, refrained from giving a "particular description of it," since he considered it "impossible to describe it bad enough."[4] Early in 1765 the *London Chronicle* quoted from a pamphlet, "With respect to East Florida, it has been so much the subject of conversation, ridicule, and dispute, that it is difficult to form any very certain ideas concerning it."[5] On the whole, however, Florida was thought to be a land of possibilities, but one which needed settlers before they could be realized.

Of Canada, the third great region added to the empire as a result of the war, much less was heard. The greatest in-

---

[1] *S. J. C.*, Sept. 20, 1764; see *Lloyd's E. P.*, Feb. 6, 1765; *L. C., Aug.* 25, 1764; *London Mag.*, March, 1765, p. 120.

[2] *L. C.*, Sept. 8, 1764.

[3] *L. C.*, Jan. 31, 1765.

[4] *Gent. Mag.*, Feb., 1765; see *S. J. C.*, Feb. 2, 1765.

[5] *L. C.*, Feb. 23, 1765; see a series of eight letters, "The American Police," beginning in the *Gaz.*, Oct. 13, 1767.

terest shown in that acquisition was in regard to the Canada Bills, as the paper money there was usually called. There were almost seventeen million livres of French paper money circulating in Canada in 1764 [1] and the holders of these bills were fearful lest they become worthless. Apparently, some speculation had been carried on in them, for some holders, because of this fear, had sold at a low price. In the peace of 1763 arrangements had been made about them with the French government, but as the French were very dilatory in fulfilling their part of the agreement, persistent negotiations were necessary before any payments were made. Frequent newspaper mention showed that the holders were much disturbed over the slowness of the French. [2]

We have seen what " Candidus " thought of the prospects of the colonies. [3] He was not alone in his opinion. Especially when the Stamp Act troubles began to become important, writers were not lacking to inform Englishmen of the hazards of affronting America because of her great possibilities and glorious future, which some day would make her too powerful to be ruled by force. Thomas Pownall had told of the great future of America in a pamphlet, The Administration of the Colonies, which was widely noticed in the papers. [4]   " Rationalis " wrote, " Little doubt can be entertained, that this vast country will in time become the greatest and most prosperous empire that perhaps the world has ever seen." He thought the population would

[1] Can. Arch. Q., 2, p. 168.

[2] See Kingsford, Hist. of Can. (London, 1892), vol. iv, pp. 458-461; vol. v, pp. 179-182; see London E. P., Aug. 10, 1765; P. A., Sept. 3, 1765; L. C., Jan. 5, 1765; S. J. C., May 16, 1765.

[3] Supra, pp. 39-40.

[4] This was first printed in 1764 as a pamphlet of 131 pages and was subsequently several times enlarged until it reached 610 pages in 1774; see C. W. A. Pownall, Thomas Pownall (London, 1908), p. 181.

double every twenty-five years, and that by 1865 the population of America would be thirty-two millions. True
policy, he said, not a policy of coercion, must be the tie to
hold them to England.[1] The views he expressed were not
uncommon.

In 1763 the British ministry evolved a three-fold plan for
stricter colonial control. They proposed, first, to enforce
vigorously the acts of trade and navigation, some of which
had so long been evaded by colonial smugglers that many
traders seemed to think they had a right to such illicit trade
without interruption; second, to raise a revenue in the colonies; and third, to use this revenue to support British troops
in America. The efforts to enforce the navigation laws by
giving new powers to vice-admiralty courts and naval officers in America led to endless bickerings, resentment and
interference with trade. The Sugar Act of 1764 put many
restrictions on the West Indian trade, and halved the duty
on molasses imported into the continental colonies from
other than British islands. Since the Molasses Act of 1733,
which had put a prohibitory duty on such molasses, was
practically a dead letter, the colonists did not object to it;
but this new duty was to be carefully collected; there was
the rub. These acts, which cramped, or made impossible,
colonial trade with the French and Spanish West Indies,
were very injurious to the colonial commerce, for molasses
especially had been a very important item in the trade cycle
of the northern colonies. It was from this trade, too, that
the colonists got much of their hard cash, and the cutting
off of this supply, added to the concurrent prohibition of
paper money, was a very considerable grievance.[2]

Extracts from the Sugar Act were widely printed in Eng-

---

[1] *London Mag.*, Nov., 1765; *L. C.*, Nov. 2, 1765; see *P. L.*, Oct. 31, 1765.

[2] See a discussion and bibliography in Howard, *Preliminaries of the
American Revolution*.

lish papers, and soon after word of it reached America, colonial reactions began to be noticed. It became law on April 5, 1764, and went into effect on September 29, 1764. A *London Chronicle* paragraph reported on September 1, 1764, that very strong remonstrances had arrived from the colonies " with respect to their crampt trade." [1] The next number reported, "They write from Bristol, that the principal merchants of that city intend to support with all their interest the independent free trade of the North American colonies." The recent restrictions were spoken of as unnatural, and it was predicted that if they were not removed soon, melancholy consequences would attend.[2] A little later an extract of a letter from New England told of the hard times prevailing there; money was scarce, trade to the French and Spanish islands was stopped, men-of-war being stationed along the coast for that purpose; murmurings and lawsuits were the rule.[3] A report in the *Gentleman's Magazine* said, " The New Commercial regulations in *North-America* are complained of as grievous to the colonies. Every king's ship is a *Guarducosta* [sic], and every cargo of the *American* product is deemed prohibited goods." This article went on to tell how important the hampered trade was and how serious the results of its stoppage would be.[4] Extracts of letters from New York and the New England colonies reported great dissatisfaction with the new regulations.[5] On September 1, the Bostonians adopted some non-importation regulations and the *London Chronicle* and other papers reported the action with care.[6] By the latter part of

[1] *L. C.*, Sept. 1, 1764.
[2] *L. C.*, Sept. 4, 1764.
[3] *L. C.*, Sept. 22, 1764.
[4] *Gent. Mag.*, Sept., 1764, p. 493; see *P. L.*, Aug. 26, 1765.
[5] *L. C.*, Jan. 29, 1765; *S. J. C.*, Oct. 4 and Dec. 11, 1764.
[6] *L. C.*, Oct. 18, Nov. 29, 1764; March 9, 1765.

1764 English readers knew that the Sugar Act was unpopular in America and they knew the reasons for its unpopularity, but there is little evidence to show that they regarded the situation as at all serious.

With the coming of the year 1765, there were some persons who felt that the colonies were being subjected to severe treatment. "Mercator" sent to the *St. James's Chronicle* a letter from Boston which ably presented the American side of the case. In his introduction he said it was upon a "Subject of the utmost Importance both to our Colonies and the Mother Country." If great care were not taken he was afraid the colonists would be *" forced into a state of Independence."* Then the people of Great Britain would be sorry for having trusted so much to " West India Influence in the Senate." [1] News of the bad condition of trade in America, due to the trade regulations and the Currency Act, appeared with greater frequency, and the English public began to be dimly aware that all was not well beyond the Atlantic.

The Currency Act of 1764 was much commented upon. It was entitled, " An Act to prevent paper Bills of Credit,

[1] *S. J. C.,* Jan. 17, 1765; see an interesting article on West Indian influence in parliament, *Gent. Mag.,* May, 1766. The West Indies were so highly valued then that " A Dutiful Subject " said " the islands are by far the richest and most considerable part of America. The continentalists are mere beggars, compared with the inhabitants of the islands. Jamaica alone contains more riches than the whole continent of North America. . . . For this reason it is evident, that the islands are entitled to our most respectable regards." *Gaz.,* Feb. 18, 1766. Another letter said that the new regulations " seem to have had their rise from the West Indies." *P. L.,* Sept. 10, 1765; see *P. L.,* Sept. 14, 23, 1765. " An Impartial Bystander " said, " If I am not misinformed, there are now in parliament upwards of 40 members who are either West India planters themselves, descended from such, or have concerns there that entitle them to this preeminence." *Gaz.,* May 5, 1766. " Britanicus " said that Grenville took measures against the Americans " to please some members concerned in the Sugar islands." *Gaz.,* March 26, 1767; see Jan. 18, 1766; see an article in the *English Hist. Review,* July, 1921.

hereafter to be issued in any of His Majesty's colonies or plantations in America, from being declared to be a legal tender in payments of money; and to prevent the legal tender of such bills as are now subsisting from being prolonged beyond the periods limited for calling in and sinking the same." The advocates of this bill claimed that it would lessen confusion and improve credit in the colonies. The opponents pointed out that it worked a real hardship on colonies where specie was scarce.

In April, 1764, a *St. James's Chronicle* paragraph stated that, though it might be beneficial to establish a real currency in America, yet at first setting out " to call in the Paper Money so long used," would be " attended with difficulties almost insuperable. . . ." [1] Before the end of the year many notices of the currency situation in the colonies were printed. "Tim Hint" noted that there had " long been great Complaints for Want of Coin in common Currency in North America " and submitted a plan for introducing copper money. [2] A paragraph reported, " So great is the scarcity of cash in the colonies, that, we are assured, in all the plantations together, they could not raise 300,000 £." [3] A gentleman lately returned from New York reported cash so scarce in that city " and bills on London so difficult to procure, that he was obliged to give eight guineas premium for a bill of 100 £ sterling." [4] " Rationalis," in a widely printed letter, advised that the Americans be allowed to keep their paper money in order that they might send their bullion to England. What difference did it make, he asked, as long as England continued to get all of America's real wealth. [5] A sceptical Englishman, on the other hand, after

[1] *S. J. C.*, April 21, 1764.

[2] *S. J. C.*, March 26, 1765.

[3] *Lloyd's E. P.*, Nov. 4, 1765.

[4] *L. C.*, Dec. 7, 1765.

[5] *London Mag.*, Nov., 1765, p. 573.

citing some large racing purses offered in Philadelphia, said the Americans were only representing that they were in financial difficulties " to cover their unwillingness to pay towards their own support. . . ." [1]

A little comment was caused by the project of quartering troops in America.[2] " M " opposed such action because it might be but an opening wedge, the establishment of a precedent, which would ultimately react against the liberties of England.[3] A committee of North American merchants gave an entertainment at the King's Arms Tavern in Cornhill to Richard Glover and Charles Garth for " their zealous endeavours and ready assistance in the last Session of Parliament to prevent the soldiery from being billeted upon the private houses of their fellow-subjects in America." [4] "An American " objected to the quartering of troops because he thought the colonists should be allowed the " privilege of axing themselves." [5]

Though the majority of Englishmen were probably little concerned with colonial objections to acts that were being enforced on the far side of the Atlantic, there were some who took a very keen interest in such affairs. They were first of all the merchants and second the manufacturers, and the papers were not remiss in supplying information for

[1] *Lloyd's E. P.,* Nov. 21, 1764.

[2] The Quartering Act of 1765 required the provinces to provide quarters and certain specified necessities for the troops the home government stationed among them. This required some expenditure and was therefore tantamount to taxation. The Act was not a surprise to the colonists as they had known of it as a possibility for some time. For the act see MacDonald, *Select Charters,* p. 306.

[3] *S. J. C.,* April 18, 1765.

[4] *Lloyd's E. P.,* Aug. 16, 1765. By " American merchants " were meant merchants who traded with America, not merchants living in America or merchants from America living in England.

[5] *S. J. C.,* April 18, 1765.

them and in giving opinion representing their viewpoint. As a large share of England's commerce was with her daughter colonies, conditions that affected this trade were of great interest to increasingly influential sections of English society. This interest can be clearly seen in the press comments on the Sugar and Currency Acts. In succeeding years commercial interests were generally the predominating force governing the acts of England, and hence the student of the period must pay attention to the desires of the English merchant and manufacturer if he would understand English action.

The Sugar Act, especially, worked a hardship on English trade by cutting off much of the colonists' supply of hard cash; and the newspapers show that English merchants quickly felt the untoward effects. An extract from a New York letter said, " We could wish our Mother Country would not be so inclined to cramp us in our trade, by which alone we are enabled to make good our contracts with the Merchants at home." [1] A paragraph reported, "It has been said by those who are good judges in West-Indian affairs, that by cramping the trade with the Spaniards in America, we have already been sufferers in the sum of 100,000 hard pistoles." [2] A little later the St. James's Chronicle took note of letters from New England complaining of the restrictions and prophesying that remittances to England would become tardy and perhaps might cease altogether unless " things speedily take another Turn." [3] One paragrapher thought the cloud had a silver lining, even if the gentlemen in trade had suffered severely, for the hardships and restrictions there would " open the eyes of the kingdom to the importance of our plantations, and teach us to show some regard

[1] Lloyd's E. P., July 27, 1764.
[2] Lloyd's E. P., Aug. 29, 1764.
[3] S. J. C., Sept. 6, 1764.

for the interest of those places which we thought it worth our while to purchase with millions of money, and oceans of blood." [1] Upon this prophecy which, indeed, seemed eminently reasonable, future events were a sad commentary.

"Rationalis" expressed a common view when he argued that any restrictions which tended to prevent the colonies from enriching themselves by trade with foreign countries were prejudicial to the mother country, and could hurt none so much as England herself for "all the riches which they acquire, must in one shape or another, finally center among us. . . ." [2]

The manufacturers, likewise, laboring under the doctrines of mercantilism, and with a view to profits, kept a watchful eye on colonial affairs. One of the tenets of the mercantile system, which had come to be regarded as an immutable law by a great number of Englishmen, was that if the Americans should manufacture for themselves, their value to England would be lost; and therefore most Englishmen had long been jealous of any colonial attempts at manufacturing. The press of the time clearly reflected such feeling, for all through 1764 a keen interest was shown in what the Americans manufactured.

Americans sent some beautiful samples of cotton goods made in Philadelphia to London, and a paragraph reported their progress in that and other branches of manufacturing "by which it should seem, that our American colonies intend to shake off, by degrees, what they have long called a slavish dependence on the mother country." [3] Glass, linen, tin, silk, carpets, cotton goods, blankets, paper and iron were among the articles America was reported to be making.

[1] *Lloyd's E. P.,* Jan. 18, 1765.

[2] *London Mag.,* Nov., 1765 and *L. C.,* Nov. 2, 1765.

[3] *Lloyd's E. P.,* Aug. 10, 1764.

So much iron was worked up in New England that the iron exports from the mother country were reported to have fallen off £10,000 in a single year.[1] Another paragraph told of fourteen new manufactures set up in North America which were reputed to injure Great Britain " in a Sum little short of half a Million Sterling." [2]

Observers were not long in connecting the alleged increase in American manufactures with the Sugar Act and the trade regulations. Letter writers from various parts of the colonies pointed out that with the stagnation of trade in America, the colonists, unable to purchase from England, were being forced to manufacture for themselves, and that unless England changed her methods a great part of her market would be lost.[3] A widely printed letter gave one of the best summaries of the situation:

It is something remarkable, that ever since the regulations were made last year, concerning the *North American* trade, we hardly read a newspaper that does not mention manufactures of one kind or another going from *England, Scotland*, or Ireland, to settle in those colonies; which, if true, is certainly a matter that should to the last degree prove alarming to these kingdoms.[4]

The writer pointed out that if, because of the regulations, the Americans could not sell their products, they must turn to some extent from agriculture to manufacturing, which would mean that English working men would be thrown out of employment at home and would be forced to emigrate. Such, he thought, had been the effects of the late regulations,

---

[1] *Lloyd's E. P.*, Oct. 19, 1764.

[2] *Lloyd's E. P.*, Feb. 4, 1765; see *S. J. C.*, Feb. 5, 1765; *P. L.*, July 6, 1765.

[3] Letter from Virginia, *L. C.*, Oct. 30, 1764; from New England *S. J. C.*, Jan. 8, 1765; and from New York, *London Mag.*, July, 1765.

[4] In *Gent. Mag.*, Jan., 1765; *L. C.*, Jan. 15, 1765; *S. J. C.*, Feb. 5, 1765.

and as the laboring people were the strength of the country, he questioned the wisdom of such a policy and urged that great thought should be taken before these measures were allowed to stand. The papers watched with interest the formation in New York of "The Society for the Promoting of Arts, Agriculture, and Oeconomy," a society which later attained considerable prominence.[1]

Though such news and opinions as have been indicated in the last few pages can be found in the files of any representative paper of the time, it cannot be said that the papers reveal anything like a general interest in American conditions. America was at no time the leading topic, as she was at several later periods. Englishmen liked to learn of the Indians and of the new lands won during the war, and manufacturers took a rather keen interest in the recent trade regulations concerning America, for these made themselves felt in that very sensitive English nerve, the pocketbook. Not however until the Americans began to resist the Stamp Act, did the colonies win a major place in the English press.

[1] *Lloyd's E. P.*, Jan. 30 and Feb. 27, 1765; see Schlesinger, *The Colonial Merchants and the American Revolution, 1763-1776* (New York, 1917), p. 64.

CHAPTER III

THE STAMP ACT

NOTICE of the Stamp Act was given in the House of Commons on March 9, 1764, but the project was postponed until February of the following year, when the act was formally introduced into the house. On March 22, 1765, the Stamp Act received the royal assent and became law. During the interval the press contained little mention and less discussion of the act that was to prove so momentous in English and American history.

In looking for the cause of the Stamp Act one must remember the huge debt the English had piled up during the lately closed French and Indian War. This national debt both impressed and oppressed many Englishmen, and inspired frequent newspaper articles. It had been caused by the war which was generally felt to have been caused by the colonies and colonial interests. Many an Englishman would have agreed with " A West Countryman " when he wrote in the *London Chronicle,* "The cause of the late war was wholly an American one, the expenses attending which has loaded the government with an immense increase of debt." [1] With such a view commonly held, it is a little surprising that more of the discussions of the national debt, which appeared before the English realized the importance of American resistance to the Stamp Act, did not point to America as a source of revenue. Yet before the Stamp

[1] *L. C.,* Jan. 16, 1766. For other expressions of the same view see *L. C.,* Aug. 31, Oct. 31, March 7, 1775, Dec. 3, 6, 1774; *S. J. C.,* Dec. 22, 1774; see *infra* (chap. on Colonial and Imperial Thinking).

Act troubles, little mention of America as a possible revenue producer was made. After the trouble began the argument that the debt had been caused by a war undertaken in behalf of America was frequently used to justify American taxation, but this appears to have been an afterthought.

Occasionally, however, someone proposed colonial taxation in connection with the reduction of the national debt, land taxation being the favorite form advocated. In November, 1765, the *London Magazine* gave a report and discussion of the Sugar Act which had passed in April of the preceding year. The writer of the report had never a thought that the Americans would object to taxation by parliament, and was concerned only with the best method of getting revenue from them. He said he was disposed to believe that this would not be the last tax that would be " imposed by the parliament of Great-Britain upon our fellow subjects in America," and was surprised that no one had thought of the " quit rents due to the crown," at least in all the colonies that were not proprietary.[1] A land tax, he thought, had good possibilities. In the following September this magazine reported and discussed the Stamp Act in the same way.[2] Again a land tax was favored, the writer stating that he must think " that the extending of the land-tax to the British dominions in America was, in many respects, preferable to the taxes that have been lately imposed upon them." [3] Letters from America suggesting a land tax were printed in the *London Magazine* and the *St. James's Chronicle.*[4] A

[1] *London Mag.*, Nov., 1764, pp. 555-558. This writer was in error as quit-rents were not a source of revenue in the New England Colonies.

[2] During these first years several months always elapsed before parliamentary reports were printed.

[3] *London Mag.*, Sept., 1765, p. 450.

[4] *London Mag.*, July, 1765, p. 372; *S. J. C.,* July 6, 1765.

paragraph in the latter said, "We hear a Scheme for introducing an equitable Land-tax in the North American Colonies is now under Consideration, in Consequence of some late Appeals sent over from the principal Provinces." [1]

The Stamp Act itself was mentioned only occasionally. A *London Magazine* writer thought customs duties likely to be very costly and hard to collect in a country where smuggling was so prevalent and where juries would be so reluctant to convict as in America. A stamp tax might have been collected with ease, but though one had been proposed the preceding March, it had not yet been enacted.[2] A letter from Providence, Rhode Island was printed, reporting an address of the Rhode Island Assembly to the King in which it prayed " that Stamp Duties and Internal Taxes be not laid on the People here without their own Consent." [3] Infrequent paragraphs served to notify the observant reader that there was a proposal to lay a stamp act on America. In November, 1764, a *Lloyd's Evening Post* paragraph informed the public that " a scheme for imposing a general stamp duty in North America is now finished," [4] but a month later another paragraph reported that a stamp duty, having " been found impracticable as to the mode of collection in that country, is now laid aside." [5] In February a one-sentence paragraph went the rounds of the papers to the effect that such an act was sure to pass, as the plantation agents had failed in their opposition to it, and that the stamp commissioners were to be natives of the provinces where the tax was to be collected.[6]

---

[1] *S. J. C.*, July 16, 1765; see *P. L.*, Aug. 19, 1765.

[2] *London Mag.*, Sept., 1764, p. 449.

[3] *S. J. C.*, Jan. 17, 1765.

[4] *Lloyd's E. P.*, Nov. 9, 1764.

[5] *Lloyd's E. P.*, Dec. 19, 1764.

[6] *L. C.*, Feb. 19, 1765.

In September, long after the act had passed, but before its significance was realized, the *London Magazine* recorder of parliamentary proceedings thought it worth while to report the presentation of petitions against the act at the time of its passing, by agents of Virginia, South Carolina and Connecticut.[1]   Names of the stamp officers for the various colonies were occasionally printed, but without comment.[2]   Thus, though there was some slight mention of American taxation in the English publications before the act became law, there was no realization of its significance at all commensurate with the importance which coming events were to give to the question.   No reader not endowed with the gift of prophecy could have predicted that the act was to stir up a mighty storm.   In this failure to appreciate the significance of the attempt to tax the colonies, the press was at one with parliament itself, for the very body that passed the legislation did so in the most perfunctory way.

During the first few months after March 22, 1765, the press was nearly as far from recognizing the trouble the act was to cause as it was during the months preceding its passage.   About the first of June news that might have been disquieting began to come from across the Atlantic.   The *St. James's Chronicle* printed extracts from New York letters telling of the early reception of the Stamp Act news in that city, where it was cried about the streets and called *" The Folly of England and the Ruin of America."* [3]   The colonists were said to be greatly alarmed.   The merchants trading to America were alleged to have lost large orders "countermanded, on account of the new American Stamp Duties." [4] American printers were reported to be making plans to dis-

[1] *London Mag.*, Sept., 1765, p. 447.
[2] *P. L.*, July 29, 1765.
[3] *S. J. C.*, June 6, 1765; see *P. L.*, Aug. 12, 1765.
[4] *S. J. C.*, June 8, 1765.

continue or curtail publication on account of the tax.[1] These accounts, however, were but straws, and it is clear that no great thought was given to the situation. None of the papers gave much material on the subject, and even the leading ones often printed several consecutive issues with no mention whatever of the Stamp Act.

Increasingly, however, as the months went by, the seriousness of the situation became apparent. An important expression of American opinion was the set of resolutions, some of which were passed and some only drawn up, by the Virginia House of Burgesses, May 29, 1765. The *London Magazine* and the *Universal Magazine* reported their " several warm and extraordinary resolutions relative to the stamp duty " which concluded with the resolve, " ' That any person who shall, by speaking or writing, maintain that any person or persons, other than the general assembly of that colony, have any right or power to impose any taxation whatever on the people there, shall be deemed enemies to that, his majesty's colony.' " [2] These resolutions quickly drew comment and letters of opposition, several of which, signed " William Pym," were printed in the *Public Ledger*.[3] "A Virginian " also attacked the resolutions.[4] " Bristoliensis " in turn opposed the arguments of "A Virginian." [5] Early harbingers of the great controversy which was soon to rage were appearing; the letter writers were beginning to take sides on the American question.

Probably the earliest newspaper discussion of the general issues involved was in two letters signed "Marcus Aurelius,"

[1] *S. J. C.*, July 18, 1765; Aug. 3, 1765; *L. C.*, July 13, 1765; *Lloyd's E. P.*, July 15, 17, 1765; *P. L.*, July 18, 1765.

[2] *London Mag.*, Aug., 1765, p. 433; *Univ. Mag.*, Aug., 1765, p. 107.

[3] *P. L.*, Aug. 13, 19, 26, 30, 1765; see *Lloyd's E. P.*, Aug. 14, 21, 1765.

[4] *Lloyd's E. P.*, Sept. 2, 1765.

[5] *Lloyd's E. P.*, Oct. 30, 1765.

called *A Dialogue Between an American and a Courtier.* In the first letter the Courtier argued that taxation of America was right, because the Americans were subjects, because England had repeatedly succored them in time of war, and because England had nursed America in her infancy. Therefore America, now that she had grown up, should aid the mother country. The American acknowledged that the colonists were subjects, but claimed that they could not be taxed lawfully without representation. As to the succor England had extended in past wars, it was motivated by self-interest; and, besides, America had borne her full share of defense. He denied that America had been nursed in her infancy, claiming that the early inhabitants had fled from tyranny in England. In the second letter the Courtier asked if it was not reasonable that America should be taxed for her own defense, to which the American replied that it was and that this was already being done by the representatives of every colony. But the Courtier thought the Americans should be taxed for the upkeep of the army sent to defend them, to which the American emphatically answered that the colonists neither needed nor wanted that army.[1] Surely, observed the Courtier, the Americans valued the protection of the British navy and should help to pay for it. Quite right, retorted the American, but claimed that they did pay handsomely by using great quantities of heavily-taxed English goods. The Courtier was convinced, and upon learning that the Americans objected to taxes on sugar and molasses and to the Stamp Act, promised to use his influence to have them repealed.[2] This significant and comprehensive dialogue appeared, however, sometime before there was a general discussion.

[1] *Cf. infra*, pp. 61, 70.

[2] *L. C.*, Aug. 17, 27, 1765; also in *London E. P.*, Aug. 17 and in the *P. L.* at about the same time.

The tempo quickened. From the latter part of August, 1765, onward, the greater frequency of paragraphs, letters and articles showed that the English press was becoming aware of difficulties over the Stamp Act. The colonists were showing their displeasure in more certain tones. At last the Boston riots of August, which reached their most spectacular point in the sack of Lieutenant-Governor Hutchinson's house and the burning of his effects, brought home to the English public the realization of serious trouble in America. The *Public Ledger* printed an account of these disorders on October 10. On October 18, *Lloyd's Evening Post* published a four-column report of the riots, the printer prefacing his account, taken directly from American letters and papers, with a few remarks on the prodigious height reached by the spirit of the colonists, acknowledging his duty to give "every information in our power relative to the excesses " and begging that the readers would " excuse the length of the following articles on account of the subject." [1] The *St. James's Chronicle* prefaced a letter on the riots with the remark that it was desired because of the " present Melancholy Situation of Affairs with Respect to the Colonies and the Mother Country." [2] The *Universal Magazine* printed nearly three pages on the situation and, like *Lloyd's Evening Post,* thought it necessary to apologize for the length of the account! It hoped that readers would excuse the unusual length since the trouble in America was so great that every possible bit of information must be given. [3] The accounts were continued from month to month in the various magazines, the *Universal Magazine* promising to give its readers " all Accounts regularly till this interesting Affair is decided." [4] From the middle of October, 1765, through

[1] *Lloyd's E. P.,* Oct. 18, 1765.
[2] *S. J. C.,* Oct. 22, 1765.
[3] *Universal Mag.,* Oct., 1765, pp. 216-218.
[4] *Universal Mag.,* Supplement, 1765, p. 375.

the rest of that year and well into 1766, the Stamp Act was by far the leading topic of English journalism. As " A Lancastrian " said, the American troubles were " the general Topic of most Persons and Papers." [1] The papers followed events closely, and considering the limitations of eighteenth-century journalism, which among other things made reports from America habitually from four to six weeks late, they reported American events very well. Letters for or against the act began to pour in; sometimes the colonies were criticized for their hasty action, and sometimes they were praised. The press revealed a general realization of a serious situation.

Information from America was received and distributed in three ways. First, accounts were taken from American papers in entirety or in extract. Rarely were they condensed or rewritten. Second, letters or extracts from American letters were printed. Third, state papers were given. Thus the frequent disputes which Massachusetts had with its governors throughout the period and the messages back and forth were carefully given. The names of Bernard and Hutchinson appeared frequently in the papers. Figures from two representative papers will serve to indicate the space American views and reports received during the Stamp Act troubles. The *Gentleman's Magazine* averaged about fifty-two pages in each issue. In January, 1766, seven and a half pages were given to America; in February, nine and a half; in March, five and a half; and in April, seven. The *London Chronicle,* a tri-weekly paper, averaged about seventeen columns in each issue, exclusive of advertising. On March sixth it gave about three columns to America; the eighth, three; the eleventh, two; the thirteenth, two and a quarter. The proportions are typical during the Stamp Act troubles.

[1] *S. J. C.,* Feb. 8, 1766.

The papers remembered their professions of impartiality, and no American could reasonably claim it was not observed. The *Gentleman's Magazine,* after giving a summary of the arguments against repeal, at the end of the article promised:

We shall in some future Magazine collect the arguments for the repeal of the Stamp-Act, as it is by no means our intention to espouse one side of the question; but to represent impartially the arguments on both sides, that our readers being fully informed of all that have been urged, may judge of the force of each, and form his own private judgment accordingly.[1]

The *London Chronicle* gathered into one article the leading arguments for and against the act under the heading,. " A short Sketch of the Arguments for and Against the American Stamp Act." [2]   The entire English press speedily became an open forum and in its columns the first great contest over American policy was soon raging. It was but the opening chapter of a great debate that lasted until the war of words was over and the sword was unsheathed to give the decision.

Together with the arguments of expediency, the Stamp Act released a flood of legal and constitutional argument. As after-events were to prove, these issues were not met and settled at the time, but were only patched over by a repeal accompanied by the Declaratory Act asserting parliamentary right to legislate for the colonies " in all cases whatsoever." The issues of taxation and representation, which involved searchings into the nature of the English constitution, continued to be discussed throughout the whole period. Constitutional arguments will be deferred for later consideration, while other arguments over the Stamp Act are followed through to the time of its repeal.

[1] *Gent. Mag.,* March, 1766.
[2] *L. C.,* Jan. 21, 1766.

The possibility of repealing the obnoxious legislation soon became apparent. Aside from the constitutional or legal arguments, the advocates of repeal based their opposition to the act on the broad grounds of expediency.[1] The Stamp Act should be set aside: first, because it was injurious to British trade; second, because it irritated a people who were becoming so strong that coercive measures would in brief time be of no avail, at which time England would wish that a policy of friendship based upon mutual advantage had been pursued; third, because by means of trade regulation England already had a recognized way of getting sufficient money from the colonies; fourth, because a system of requisitions would have raised the same amount of money in a less irritating way; and fifth, because the protecting army, for whose support the tax had been levied, was neither needed or desired, since the Americans were well able to take care of themselves.

The opponents of repeal, always, of course, maintaining the constitutionality of the act, supported it on the ground, first, that America should help to bear some of the burden that had been and was being incurred in her defense,[2] commonly using the analogy of England, the mother, and America, the child, who had become ungrateful despite the many advantages showered upon her. Second, they insisted that repeal would hurt the dignity and authority of England; the measure, once having been passed, must be enforced, or all authority for the future would be lost. Third, and closely allied to the second reason, they alleged that the American objections against the Stamp Act were equally good against all laws whatsoever made by the home country, and hence

[1] See for example *S. J. C.*, Feb. 1, 1766; *Lloyd's E. P.*, Dec. 6, 1765.

[2] Occasionally some seemed to think that America should be taxed to pay the national debt; see *Gaz.*, Jan. 24, 1766, Sept. 28, 1768; *P. L.*, Oct. 4, 1765.

that if the Stamp Act were given up the colonies would soon become practically independent. Fourth, they argued that the tax was very light and that America could afford to pay.

The American reactions to the act had not long been known in England before significant items of commercial and manufacturing interest began to appear in the papers. A *London Chronicle* paragraph informed its readers that manufactures were daily increasing in Pennsylvania. Homespun, superior to any cloth made in England, was being produced;[1] while other manufactures were reported to be stimulated by the act.[2] This was alleged to be largely for two reasons: first, the Americans, foreseeing that they would be drained of their specie by the act and thus would be unable to buy goods, were beginning to manufacture for themselves; and second, they were so irritated that non-importation, non-use of British manufactures and use of goods made at home was becoming a patriotic duty. A *St. James's Chronicle* paragraph reported a falling off in exports to America, which were calculated at " near 600,000 £. less this Summer, than has been known for 30 years past." [3] Shipments, conditional on the repeal of the act, began to be reported, Boston sending large orders with that proviso.[4] Orders countermanded on account of the duty were reported to amount to 700,000 sterling,[5] and it was expected that large quantities of hats sent to Boston and Philadelphia would be returned.[6] Merchant ships in the Thames were reported to be laid up, with crews discharged, until the fate

[1] *L. C.,* Jan. 28, 1766.
[2] *L. C.,* Feb. 20, 1766.
[3] *S. J. C.,* Oct. 26, 1765; *Lloyd's E. P.,* Oct. 28, 1765.
[4] *Lloyd's E. P.,* Nov. 25, 1765; *Gaz.,* Jan. 28, 1766.
[5] *S. J. C.,* Dec. 14, 1766.
[6] *W. E. P.,* Feb. 13, 1766.

of the Stamp Act should be decided.[1] Shipwrights, caulkers and workers in every branch of the shipping business were reported to be out of work.[2] An "Exact computation" appeared in the papers stating that British profits from the American trade had been upwards of £2,000,000 annually since the war closed but now this trade was in process of being ruined.[3] A paragraph of wide circulation told that the Americans owed to the merchants of Great Britain and Ireland "upwards of Four Million Sterling." [4] Some feared that the colonists would not be able to pay this debt and others intimated that the disturbances would furnish an excuse for defaulting. Home manufacturers were reported to be on the verge of ruin, one stocking manufacturer near London being forced to discharge no less than forty workmen because of the act.[5] Black cloth was returned from America as the colonists were "determined not to wear any mourning." [6]

" Fear Not " wrote a letter stating it as a truth which could not be denied that " our Colonies are in the utmost Distress, our Trade almost gone, and our Manufactures almost ruined." [7] "Amicus," savagely attacking the enemies of repeal, wrote from Norwich that his large trade to America had been ruined by the Stamp Act and his workingmen were suffering grievously.[8] The *London Magazine* printed a long article from Birmingham in which the writer set forth the importance of the American trade and the suffering

[1] *W. E. P.*, Feb. 4, 1766; see *Lloyd's E. P.*, Feb. 3, 1766.

[2] *S. J. C.*, Jan. 9, 1766.

[3] *Lloyd's E. P.*, May 16, 1766.

[4] *S. J. C.*, Feb. 15, 1766.

[5] *S. J. C.*, Jan. 9, 1766.

[6] *S. J. C.*, Feb. 13, 1766.

[7] *S. J. C.*, Jan. 30, 1766.

[8] *Lloyd's E. P.*, March 7, 1766.

that had accompanied its interruption. The working poor, he asserted, would be the worst sufferers. Attempting to forestall the argument that he was writing from selfish motives, this advocate of repeal, who appeared to be an iron manufacturer, argued that the crisis was of great importance to the entire community. He used no legal arguments, he presented no plan, but he earnestly requested that something be done.[1] The *Gentleman's Magazine* reported that merchants trading to North America had met and considered measures to be taken, among which a petition to Parliament for repeal was prominent.[2] Early in February, 1766, paragraphs mentioned that petitions from manufacturers had been sent to Parliament asking for repeal, but at the time these petitions did not get more than a passing mention. The convention, which made it obligatory for papers to wait several months before reporting proceedings in Parliament, saw to that. In September, however, the *London Magazine* reported numerous petitions that had been presented January 17 and 28. Organizations, mostly of merchants and manufacturers, from London, Bristol, Liverpool, Halifax, Lancaster, Manchester, Leicester, Bradford, Frome, Birmingham, Coventry, Macclesfield, Woolverhampton, Stourbridge, Dudley, Minehead, Taunton, Witney, Newcastle-upon-Tyne, Glasgow, Chippenham and Nottingham petitioned, "all complaining of the great decay in trade to the North American colonies, owing to the late obstructions and embarrassments laid thereon, and praying for relief."[3] Though these petitions did not get into the magazines until long after the act was repealed, there were items and letters enough before that step was taken to show that the merchants and manufacturers were alive to the situation and were doing what

[1] *London Mag.*, Jan., 1766.
[2] *Gent. Mag.*, Dec., 1765, p. 588.
[3] *London Mag.*, Sept., 1766, pp. 449-455.

they could to protect their interests. Petitions from America likewise were received, but these carried less weight than those from home interests.[1]

Efforts were made to interest the governing class of English society by an appeal to their interests. "Vox Populi" urged repeal, first, because otherwise trade would be ruined. Merchants, he said, were trembling: people in trade were groaning at approaching ruin; the laboring poor lived in expectation of famine and desolation. Then he addressed himself to the landed interest, whom he knew to be the chief rulers of England. "And oh, ye opulent guardians of us all! what can you foresee but the destruction of your estates for want of culture."[2] Another letter writer, using the favorite form of queries, tried to show that the approaching ruin would strike all classes of Englishmen. Trade and commerce would suffer and workmen would lose their employment. Then he asked in successive queries: " 4 Must not the Burthen of maintaining them chiefly fall on those of the landed interest?" " 5 Must not the deficiencies of Taxes occasioned by their Ruin, be principally made good by the landed Gentlemen?" and " 6 In what degree will landed Property become affected, by such a Dimunition of People as from the Loss of that Trade will be occasioned?"[3] "Rationalis" warned, "above all things, the Landed Interest must not be favoured at the expence of the Commercial . . . for, in fact, the Landed Interest can really be only supported by the prosperity of Commerce."[4] Such attempts to enlist the landed interest on the side of repeal were not frequent, but they were indicative of a significant cleavage of interests in English social life.

[1] *L. C.*, Feb. 6, 1766.
[2] *L. C.*, Feb. 6, 1766.
[3] *S. J. C.*, Jan. 30, 1766; also in *Gaz.*, Jan. 29, 1766.
[4] *L. C.*, Nov. 9, 1765; see *L. C.*, March 8, 1766.

" Rationalis," a believer in the old imperial motto *divide et impera* (divide and rule), who wrote much in favor of repeal at this time, carefully pointed out the dangers to England from irritation of the Americans. He asserted he had never been in the colonies, nor had any special connection with them, and so he did not undertake to " plead partially " in their behalf; but endeavored to regulate his thoughts " by the principles of right policy." Whoever " Rationalis " was, despite his lack of close connections with America, he had views of American policy which coming events proved to be essentially sound. On October 24, 1765, when the papers were just beginning to realize the importance of the American situation, he wrote that wise men instructed by common sense had long said that Great Britain's greatest security in her North American colonies " with their progressive increase of strength from population, would be found in their disunion, from rival interests and their discordant religious principles." Because of this nothing was to be so much dreaded as an establishment of harmony among them. " But what would never probably be effected among themselves is likely to be accomplished by an ill-judged measure of the mother country's to involve them in a common calamity of oppression." [1] He repeated the warning in November, urging the English people to consider the great increase in colonial population [2] before provoking the Americans too far.

The Stamp Act Congress at New York, in October, 1765, received scarcely any contemporary mention in American papers [3] and very little in the English press, but "Rationalis" was a keen observer and its true significance did not escape him. In a letter printed in the *London Magazine* he noted

[1] *L. C.,* Oct. 24, 1765. He also wrote in *P. L.* at this time.
[2] *L. C.,* Nov. 2, 1765.
[3] Schlesinger, *op. cit.,* p. 75.

the irritating effect of the late measures in America and warned Englishmen that Americans were beginning to think:

they must unite in their own defence. They accordingly cry out for a union: and we even see, by the public papers, that there is to be a conference, or congress of deputies for that purpose, which is first proposed for representation only; but should they not therein succeed, ought we not to be aware of what they may next proceed to consult on, and what may be the consequences of either rooted hatred, or rash desperation?

He would applaud, he said, every relaxation for restoring harmony between England and her daughter.[1]

The third argument against the Stamp Act is best illustrated by an anecdote of Walpole which was printed in nearly every publication of note sometime during the American troubles. The anecdote relates that Sir Robert Walpole had been approached during the Spanish War with a scheme to tax America. "I will leave that," he is reported to have said, "for some of my successors, who may have more courage than I have and [sic] less a friend to commerce than I am." He added that it had been a maxim with him to encourage colonial trade to the utmost, indeed he had overlooked irregularities in it, for if by their commerce "they gain 500,000 £." he said he was convinced "that in two years afterwards full 250,000 £. of their gains" would be "in his majesty's exchequer by the labor and product of this kingdom. . . ." This was due to trade conditions which quickly brought a large share of America's trade gains to England. The anecdote finished by quoting him as saying, "This is taxing them more agreeably both to their own constitution and to ours."[2]   "Rationalis" was also of this

---

[1] *London Mag.*, Nov., 1765; see *L. C.*, Oct. 19, 1765; *Gaz.*, Aug. 16, 1769.

[2] See it in *London Mag.*, Dec., 1765; *L. C.*, Dec. 5, 1765; *Univ. Mag.*, Nov., 1766; *S. J. C.*, June 25, 1766; *L. P.*, June 8, 1774; *Lloyd's E. P.*, Dec. 4, 1765; *P. L.*, Dec. 6, 1765; *London E. P.*, Dec. 7, 1765; *Ipswich Journal*, Dec. 7, 1765.

opinion, thinking levying of taxes bad policy, " for if they have not money to pay them, and also to purchase our manufactures, whatever is gained in one way, must be lost to us in another." [1] With variations, this was one of the most common arguments. One of the variations was that the Americans were already heavily taxed because they used British goods which had paid a duty in England, which duty was in reality paid by the Americans because all taxes were allowed to " terminate ultimately upon the consumer." [2] This, thought some, taken in connection with the fact that American trade was so regulated that the Americans were obliged to do much of their buying and selling in the mother country, should give England the opportunity to impose sufficient indirect taxes. Duties on imports and exports would be enough. [3] "A Whig" voiced the common argument that trade taxes were enough; so why seek to impose direct taxes. [4]

" Philocles " thought that the tax was to be raised and remitted in specie and said this was the great cause of the American discontent, for it was sure to exhaust them of ready cash in a short time. [5] " Philocolonas," harking back to antiquity, reminded his readers that the " rigour of ancient *Athens* to her colonies, brought on the ruin of that noble republic " and pointed out that England had more than one Macedon at hand to take advantage of any mistakes she might make. [6] This fear of enemies closer than America gave point to an anecdote of a French nobleman, who, when asked if Frenchmen had heard of the Stamp Act

[1] *London Mag.,* Nov., 1765, p. 573.

[2] *L. C.,* March 6, 1766; *Lloyd's E. P.,* March 10, 1766.

[3] *Gent. Mag.,* Dec., 1765.

[4] *L. C.,* March 22, 1766.

[5] *Lloyd's E. P.,* Feb. 19, 1766; see May 22, 1769.

[6] *L. C.,* Feb. 15, 1766.

and American reactions to it, replied that they had, and were in great fear about it. When pressed to tell why Frenchmen should be in fear about such a matter he was reported to have said, " Monsieur, nous craignons que l'Angleterre s'accomodera trop tot avec ses colonies." [Sir, we fear that England will come to terms too quickly with her colonies.] [1] However, fear of intervention from France or Spain was expressed seldom at this period, although it was frequently at later periods.

Some friend of conciliation with the colonies caused a warning to be prominently printed in several of the papers, not only when the Stamp Act troubles were at their highest, but later, whenever friction developed between England and her colonies. This warning, which first appeared in the *London Chronicle* on November 19, 1765, and in many succeeding numbers, ran as follows:

" To Whom it May Concern, Men of England, The Colonies, Bretheren

" Consider well the *Reverse* of a Dutch medal, struck in their early troubles.

" ' Two earthen vases, floating on the waters. *Inscription.* Frangimur si collidimur.' " [2]

After the act was repealed, this notice for a time was replaced with one laudatory of Pitt.

" March XVIII, MDCCLXVI

" Englishmen, Scottishmen, Irishmen, Colonists, Bretheren.

" Rejoice in the wisdom, fortitude of *one* man, which hath saved you from civil-war and your enemies! Erect a Statue to that Man in the Metropolis of your dominions!

[1] *L. C.,* March 22, 1766.

[2] *L. C.,* Nov. 19, *passim.* It appeared in almost every issue in the latter part of 1768; see *Lloyd's E. P.,* May 2, 1770, *passim*; *P. A.,* Feb. 9, 1770, *passim*; *Gaz.,* Feb. 14, 1768.

Place a garland of oak leaves on the Pedestal, and grave
in it

Concord "[1]

An argument that was much used in the later part of the
struggle especially, was that American taxation was unnecessary because the Americans would have paid all reasonable
demands through a system of requisitions. This was a point
Franklin was very fond of advancing in his newspaper
letters. It can hardly, however, be called one of the major
arguments.[2]

"Æquus" made a clear statement of the argument that
a protecting army was not needed. He thought it very
strange that a country in peace and but lately relieved of
all real danger by the defeat and expulsion of the French,
should " *now* require a greater military force for its establishment than *lately,* when it had the enemy on its back, and
was constantly living in hot water. . . ." He also said it
was peculiar that, though this force must be supposed to be
temporary, the tax was to be made perpetual. He thought
the only enemies of America at the time were the stamps
and the distributors.[3] "Expositor," "C. T." and "A Lover
of Britain" were others who made the same argument, but
it was not very commonly advanced.[4]

While the Stamp Act repeal was in agitation, the most
prominent newspaper opponent of the American claims was
the Reverend James Scott, who wrote over the pseudonym
of "Anti-Sejanus". So prominent was he that all opponents of the repeal were not uncommonly called " Anti-
Sejanarians ". He was a prolific, audacious and scurrilous

[1] *L. C.*, March 18, 1766, *passim; Lloyd's E. P.*, March 21, 1766; *Gaz.*,
March 21, 1766.

[2] *L. C.*, Feb. 20, 1766.

[3] *L. C.*, Dec. 12, 1765.

[4] *L. C.*, Sept. 29 and *Gaz.*, Sept. 28, 1768; *L. C.*, June 22, 1765; *L. C.*,
Feb. 8, 1766 respectively.

writer, a master of invective and vituperation. As an associate of Lord Sandwich, whose chaplain he was, he became by political circumstances an opponent of repeal; and he likewise shared the odium of that dissolute lord's life. Less successful than many a wielder of the pen, he was not able to keep his identity a secret, and contemporaries sometimes attacked him with broad allusions and some of his own measure of abuse. A paragraph called him " a certain *Reverend* Gentleman," [1] another called him " a most scurrilous, profligate, priest "; [2] a *Monthly Review* writer styled him " that egregious newspaper politician." [3] He was easily the best known of the writers on his side of the question, and if we make a little allowance for the violence of his language, he was a representative one. Like many of the partisan writers of the time, especially the enemies of colonial claims, he often thought to win his point more by the vigor of his assertion than by the strength of his argument.

In one respect he was able to agree with those friendly to America, for he considered that making the stamp duties payable in specie was bad, as it would rapidly drain the Americans of their ready cash. [4] He clearly sounded the note of American ingratitude, being equally grieved and surprised at the wayward conduct of the Americans, " such an undutiful return to the mother country, for that paternal care and tenderness " with which she had fostered and protected them. To grieve and repine at so light a burden after so many kindnesses was "unnatural conduct," especially as the colonial burden was so light compared with that which England had to bear. America had been protected in the late war, she had been extended every indulgence in

[1] *L. C.*, Feb. 7, 1771.
[2] *L. P.*, April 20, 1774.
[3] *M. R.*, March, 1766, p. 239.
[4] *S. J. C.*, Dec. 3, 1765; see *Gaz.*, Feb. 18, 1765.

trade and at the present time was being protected against her enemies.[1] The argument was a common one, not only at this time but to the very end of the colonial period. " John Ploughshare " used it,[2] so did " Urban Sylvanus " [3] and many others; but it was frequently rebutted.

A *London Chronicle* writer pointed out that the Americans had assisted at the taking of Guadeloupe, Martinico and Havannah. Besides, they had helped in the reduction of Canada, and, as well as Englishmen, had involved themselves in debts they would not be able to pay for generations.[4] " X. Y. Z." refused to ascribe an altruistic role to England because of the alleged protection of America, for according to him, " If England, at an immense expence," had " protected the Americans during the late war in the enjoyment of their rights and privileges, it was for such reasons as must redound much to her own interest." [5] Neither side seems to have been convinced, for the years to come saw antagonists frequently ascribing or denying to England the part of altruism.

" Anti-Sejanus " also sounded loudly the proposition that dignity and the demands of discipline required enforcement of the act, for if " our timid and ill-judging Ministers intend to give way to the tumultous Americans," he asked, " can it be supposed that the Colonists will ever submit to bear any share in those grievous burdens and taxes, with which we are loaded?" If the colonists succeeded this time, he asserted, they would soon suffer no limitations on their trade and would shake off all dependence.[6] He ventured to

[1] *L. C.,* Jan. 28, 1766.

[2] *L. C.,* Feb. 20, 1766; see Aug. 27, 1765.

[3] *Town and Country Magazine,* Feb., 1769.

[4] *L. C.,* Feb. 20, 1766; see *K. G.,* April 20, 1774,

[5] *Lloyd's E. P.,* Jan. 24, 1766; see *L. C.,* April 11, 1767; *P. L.,* Nov. 28, 1765.

[6] *Lloyd's E. P.,* Jan. 13, 1766; see *P. A.,* Jan. 22, 1766.

state that the Stamp Act should be kept, even if it were
unreasonable and oppressive, which it was not, because of
the "riotous and illegal behaviour of the Americans, in
calling in question the right of taxation." After a time it
might be well to repeal or mitigate it, but the only immediate answer to American objections should be a rigid
enforcement.[1]

"Millions of Faithful Subjects" answered the claim so
frequently advanced by "Anti-Sejanus" and other writers,
that parliamentary dignity must be preserved, and that to
repeal the act would be to destroy it, by citing other cases
where Parliament had repealed obnoxious measures. To
some, dignity consisted in a confession of error rather than
in obstinate persistence in it.[2]

Englishmen frequently asserted that the tax was very
light upon the Americans. Paragraphers claimed that the
Americans, though a fifth in number of British subjects,
were asked to pay but a twentieth of the taxes, and chided
them for their refractoriness.[3] Another paragraph, widely
printed, even went so far as to estimate that American taxes
were but eight pence per head per annum, while in England
every person had to pay twelve shillings per annum simply
to pay interest on the debt contracted in defense of America.[4]
While this was a ridiculous misstatement, many anti-colonial
arguments of the time were based on estimates of almost
the same caliber. "Sebastian Cabot"[5] and "J. L. C.,"[6]
especially, were moved to take note of it, and not only

[1] *L. C.*, Feb. 6, 1766; see *ibid.*, Feb. 18, 1766.
[2] *S. J. C.*, Feb. 20, 1766; see *L. P.*, May 2, 1774.
[3] *London Mag.*, Oct. 1766, p. 542.
[4] *L. C.*, Feb. 1, 1766.
[5] *S. J. C.*, Feb. 6, 1766.
[6] *L. C.*, Feb. 13, 1766.

showed its absurdity but ably combated the argument that American taxation was so light as to be almost nothing.

On the whole the tone of the press during the Stamp Act period was as earnest as that during later periods of colonial unrest, but it seemed a little less factious and more spontaneous.

The 22nd of February, 1766, was a decisive day in Stamp Act history, for on that date the House of Commons by a vote of 275 to 167 gave leave to bring in a bill for the total repeal of the act.[1]   The session was long and fully attended, members pinning tickets to secure seats as early as eight in the morning.[2]   Twenty mounted men were booted and spurred ready to carry the news to all parts of England.[3] When the decisive vote was taken the papers were chary about directly reporting it.   The *Whitehall Evening Post* printed a report on February 22 that a repeal had been agreed upon, but many of the papers were silent.   The heavy hand of government was likely to fall upon those who dispensed news of Parliament before several months had elapsed.   The *St. James's Chronicle* got around the difficulty, however, by announcing, "We are assured, that the Betts now run 275 to 167, that the Stamp Act will be repealed; and it is thought that the Odds will be still higher by Monday." [4]   Twenty-four days later, on March 18, the king gave his assent to the act of repeal; the first great pre-revolutionary struggle was over.

When the Stamp Act passed few knew or cared much about it, and it was not until the reports of riotous and rebellious behavior began to come from America that the press showed any interest.   It was not so with the repeal, for in-

[1] See Howard, *op. cit.,* p. 172.

[2] *L. C.,* Feb. 25, 1766; *Lloyd's E. P.,* Feb. 24, 1766.

[3] *Lloyd's E. P.,* Feb. 24, 1766.

[4] *S. J. C.,* Feb. 22, 1766; also in *Gloucester Journal,* Feb. 24, 1766.

terest in it was long at fever heat. Even before the repeal
was definitely enacted the papers carried accounts of rejoicing in many parts of England. After the vote of February 22 the mercantile and manufacturing interests that
had been in opposition to the act gave free rein to their joy.
Reports of celebrations came in from Bristol, Liverpool,
Birmingham and Leeds, besides those that were held in
London itself.[1] Bells were rung in the towers, coffee-houses
were illuminated, bonfires were built and largess was distributed to the poor.[2]

Most of the expressions of joy, however, did not appear
till the king had given his consent on March 18. The *London Chronicle* reported that his majesty passed to and from
the House to give his assent to the bill " amidst a prodigious
concourse of people, who expressed their satisfaction for the
repeal of the Stamp-act, with the loudest exclamations of
joy." [3] The *Gentleman's Magazine* reported:

On this occasion the *American* merchants made a most numerous
appearance, to express their gratitude and joy; ships in the river
displayed their colours; houses at night were illuminated all
over the city; and every decent and orderly method was observed to demonstrate the just sense they entertained of his
majesty's goodness.[4]

Lloyd's Evening Post noted the "numerous body of
Sailors, Mechanics, &c. who gave three cheers on his Majesty's return." [5] Messengers were sent to carry the glad

[1] See *Lloyd's E. P.,* Feb. 28, March 3, 7, 1766; *S. J. C.,* March 1, 4,
1766; *W. E. P.,* March 1, 1766; *Newcastle Journal,* March 15, 1766.

[2] *S. J. C.,* Feb. 22, 1766; *L. C.,* Feb. 25, 1766; *Gaz.,* Feb. 24, 1766;
Adam's Weekly Courant, March 4, 1766.

[3] *L. C.,* March 18, 1766.

[4] *Gentleman's Mag.,* March, 1766, p. 148.

[5] *Lloyd's E. P.,* March 19, 1766.

news to "Birmingham, Sheffield, Manchester, and all the great manufacturing towns in England," and word was not long in coming back from them of the joy that was felt.[1] Bristol and Liverpool, both with large trade to America, celebrated by ringing of bells, bonfires and banquets.[2] Everywhere in England, according to the reports, the merchants and the manufacturers were rejoicing.

Notices soon appeared saying that trade had been benefited by the repeal. Upon receipt of the news more than thirty vessels were reported to have been chartered immediately for the American trade.[3] Several others set sail for America at once, some of which had been cleared out since the preceding November.[4] Large orders were reported from America: two masters only, in the shoe export trade, were said to have taken on above one hundred journeymen;[5] some hundreds of journeymen artificers in Birmingham, long unemployed, were set to work again;[6] and the repeal early began "to produce a very favourable effect upon the Funds."[7] "A Grateful Briton" exhorted merchants and manufacturers to rejoice.[8] "An Impartial Correspondent" wrote, asking the reason for all this rejoicing. He thought that the repeal had become necessary and he did not care to cry over it, but he wanted to know on what principles certain gentlemen have "ever since been testifying their joy in feasting, ringing of bells, and other acts of rejoicing."[9]

[1] *Lloyd's E. P.*, March 19, 1766; *W. E. P.*, March 20, 1766.

[2] *L. C.*, March 25, April 1, March 27, 1766; *S. J. C.*, March 27, 1766.

[3] *Lloyd's E. P.*, Feb. 28, 1766.

[4] *Lloyd's E. P.*, March 19, 1766.

[5] *L. C.* and *S. J. C.*, March 22, 1766.

[6] *S. J. C.*, March 27, 1766.

[7] *Lloyd's E. P.*, March 19, 1766.

[8] *L. C.*, March 20, 1766.

[9] *Lloyd's E. P.*, March 28, 1766; *Gaz.*, March 25, 1766.

" H." in answer, would pray inform the gentleman that, " The preservation of the *Colonies* to *Great Britain,* and the revival of the trade and navigation of these kingdoms," justified some marks of joy.[1]

The advocates of repeal were not slow in exulting over their defeated opponents, especially over " Anti-Sejanus," who had come to typify the anti-repeal party. Even before the final action a scurrilous poem of five stanzas was published, surrounded with a black border and called, "An Elegy to the *unlamented* Memory of the poor Poet, Priest, Pander, and Politician, 'Anti-Sejanus '." [2]   Several papers also printed an elaborate account of his funeral which was modeled on the funeral reports of royalty, and told with not a little delight and great detail of the procession and burial. He was buried in a criminal vault with forestallers, hogdrivers and devils in attendance. Some Americans contributed to buy a monument on which they applied to him some of his own scurrility and spoke of his " abominable Vice," " unconquerable Impudence," and "depravity of manners." [3] Truly it was the death of "Anti-Sejanus," for the Reverend Mr. Scott, probably wishing to rid himself of the burden of a defeated and thoroughly hated pseudonym, published no more letters over that signature. Other humorists took delight in writing of the funeral of Miss Ame Stamp and reported her demise with proper respect.[4]

One enthusiast over the repeal related the story of the Stamp Act in Biblical phrase and called his long and telling account, "The First Book of the Marks." The account, in three chapters, told of the sufferings of the people, of the murmurings among them, and of meetings of the Sanhedrin,

[1] *Gaz.,* March 27, 1766.
[2] *S. J. C.,* March 15, 1766.
[3] *Lloyd's E. P.,* March 12, 1766. It was widely printed.
[4] *S. J. C.,* March 20, 1766; *L. C.,* March 25, 1766.

the parliament, to consider their sufferings. A great man, Pitt, made a speech against the act and its repeal seemed assured to the people, who did then greatly rejoice. "21 And behold the music in the steeples, and on the cleavers, and on the parchments were heard throughout every street, and every alley and court." "And the instruments of wind, and the fiddle were also heard; but the bagpipe was not heard all the day long." [1] Then the elders of the people came together and cast lots to see if the marks on the papers should remain, and they numbered the Pittites and they were very great, and the marks (stamps) were to vex the people no more. Then the ruler came to give his assent and the people were exceeding glad and they " blessed him for the work of his hands." [2]

While, as was natural, the victors in the struggle were more prominent than the losers, not all of the latter were as effectively silenced as was "Anti-Sejanus." Some of them were typical "die-hards" who predicted all sorts of evil consequences from the repeal, and kept insisting that the Americans should have been forced to obey because such a concession would but make the colonists bolder in resistance.

The conclusion is irresistible to one who reads the contemporary newspapers that the Stamp Act was repealed, not because of any recognition of justice in the American claims, but because of the pressure brought to bear by the trading and manufacturing interests of England. Foreseeing their business ruined if the Stamp Act was forced upon America, they sought and gained the repeal. On March 18, a com-

---

[1] A stroke at the Scotch who were hated and almost universally represented as advocates of extreme measures against the Americans. Mansfield and Bute were the individuals most disliked.

[2] *L. C.*, March 22, 1766; see a very interesting account of the Stamp Act, also in biblical phrase in *Gaz.*, Jan. 24, 28, 29, 1766; see also *Newcastle Journal*, April 12, 1766.

mittee of London merchants wrote a letter to John Hancock and other merchants in Boston, relating the very large
part the British merchants had had in the repeal and recom-
mending to the Americans that they behave with modera-
tion, without affecting to triumph. The letter was printed in
the *Gentleman's Magazine* for September, 1766, and speedily
drew a reply from a colonist over the signature "A British
American," who thought the Americans had little reason
to exult over the action of Parliament "if (as we are told)
they acted *upon mere* commercial principles of *expedience,*
and not from those more rational ones of humanity and
justice, arising from a thorough conviction of their former
error." [1] Perhaps the merchants were overestimating their
own importance in securing the repeal, but it seems probable
that they were not.[2] In 1770 "Old Mentor," a prominent
anti-American writer, charged that the merchants had engi-
neered the whole demand for repeal, producing as evidence
what he said was a slightly imperfect copy of a letter that
a committee of merchants had written to the traders to the
colonies. The latter were instructed to write to the manufacturers from whom they got their goods, asking if there
was any slackness in trade, and if the manufacturers reported any, the merchants were informed that "you are
then to acquaint them that it is *entirely owing to the American Stamp-act,* and require them to spread that Information as wide as they can among other Manufacturers, and
to enjoin them to make use of all their Influence with Members of Parliament" for the purpose of repeal.[3] In 1775
"A Manufacturer" noted it was being alleged that the merchants had been consulted when the Stamp Act was repealed

[1] *Gent. Mag.,* Supplement, 1766, p. 612.

[2] The Declaratory Act, which was scarcely mentioned in the press is
evidence on this side.

[3] *P. A.,* Jan. 11, 1770.

and that they might try their influence again, but if they did, he hoped they would have no success.[1] The printer of the *Kentish Gazette,* after reporting the Gaspee incident in 1772, observed that the government was embarrassed by the immense influence of the vast body of merchants trading to America, and alleged that it was a melancholy truth " that in all disagreements " with the colonies these thought more of their own prosperity than of their country.[2] "A Friend to the Government " charged in 1775 that the Stamp Act was repealed " at the instance of our merchants and traders. . . ." [3]

In after years some held that the repeal had been a beneficent measure, while others said it had been pernicious. The former argued that all would have been well if England had treated the colonies in the same spirit she showed when the repeal was carried; while the latter asserted that the repeal had been interpreted in America as a sign of weakness, and hence had been the cause for presumption after presumption. "Columbus," "Matter of Fact," "Coriolanus" and "A State Tinker " were all of this way of thinking.[4]

In after years likewise the Stamp Act was commonly looked upon as the start and cause of the bitter dissensions with America, the few troubles of earlier years being crowded out of the English memory. The Stamp Act was the innovation, the new departure; from it Englishmen were wont to date the quarrel which dismembered their empire.

[1] *L. C.,* Jan. 21, 1775; see *Gaz.,* Aug. 6, 1768.

[2] *K. G.,* July 21, 1772.

[3] *K. G.,* March 29, 1775.

[4] See *P. A.,* Jan. 9, Feb. 2, 10, March 2, 1775 respectively; see *K. G.,* March 29, 1775.

CHAPTER IV

CONSTITUTIONALITY OF TAXATION

IN England, as well as in America, the cry was raised that taxation of the colonies was unconstitutional. What did Englishman mean by this complaint? In America, it is clear that some thought there was a fundamental law standing above the acts of Parliament, and that any act of Parliament contrary to this fundamental law was *ipso facto* void. Some of the Americans were basing many of their arguments not on the constitution the majority of Englishmen thought the British Empire had, but on the constitution they were thinking about, on the kind of a constitution they wanted to make, a fixed constitution which was to be fundamental law.[1] Most Englishmen, in 1765, had no such conception of their constitution.[2] To most of them the plea that a certain act was unconstitutional meant that it was contrary to custom or to the spirit of the constitution; but, if it had been passed by Parliament, it was law, which no power on earth other than that body could legally change. The accepted opinion now, as it was

[1] Josiah Tucker wrote at the time, " The Colonists reason principally from what they apprehend ought originally to be the case,—to what in future shall or must be:—and the Mother Country from what actually was,—to what still ought to be." The English based their claim on " facts and precedents," the colonists, " all the disciples of Mr. Locke have recourse to what they call immutable proofs,—the abstract reasonings, and eternal fitness of things,—and, in short, to such rights of human nature, which they suppose to be unalienable and indefeasible." This might be taken as a nut-shell statement of the whole conflict. *Universal Mag.*, Feb., 1775, p. 83.

[2] For earlier English ideas of the constitution see McIlwain, *The High Court of Parliament and Its Supremacy*, chap. ii.

in the days of George the Third, is that Parliament is legally omnipotent. Yet there is much newspaper evidence to show that the Americans, in claiming that there was a law superior to Parliament, were true to their English tradition. There were Whigs in England as well as in America who still retained the earlier English view that there was a fundamental law above Parliament, that there were general principles embodied in the English constitution before which even Parliament must bow.

"*A devoted friend to the constitution as it was settled at the revolution*," was one of these. His letter and others are worth extensive quoting.

Legislation is a derived power, therefore the whole legislative is subordinate to the end for which the power was given, namely preservation of liberty. To preserve that, it is absolutely necessary that they should not depart out of the instrument, the frame that the people when they last settled the legislative ordained. . . . To preserve the form the people have delegated the legisative in, is the primary duty of those who are called their representatives; it is, in other words, to preserve the constitution; the *whole* legislative cannot alter or change it in the essential parts. Can then that part which is the temporary, immediate representative of the people alter the constitution? Can a part have greater power than the whole? Can the representatives of the people destroy the very thing that gives them birth, the only thing by which they can be made? It is morally impossible. . . . [1]

A better statement of the American theory that the constitution is " the supreme law " would be hard to find.

"An Old Correspondent" argued that America could not be taxed because she was not represented, and in the course

[1] *London Mag.*, May, 1769, p. 260; see *Whisperer*, March 3, 1770, p. 14, *passim*.

of his argument said, " The legislative authority is not, like that of God's, absolute and reaching to all cases, but within bounds; and which if they exceed, their authority ceases, whatever power from their guns may remain." [1] " Ignotus " likewise:

The Doctrine that the supreme Power is in the Parliament, is inculcated to deceive and destroy. No such power is lodged there, as the three Bodies united are only Trustees to preserve the Constitution, not to destroy it; and as to any Imperial Sovereignty lodged there, it is a vague Assertion. The Sovereignty is in the Constitution; and should the Parliament attempt such Laws as tend to destroy the Constitution, such would be Acts of Violence, and ought to be resisted.

Continuing, he attacked the idea of passive obedience, which the Tories often implied and sometimes asserted, saying, "The impudent Assertion, that the People have no right to interfere with Government, is what the Enemies of our Constitution wish for and in Fact where Despotism resides." [2] " Demophoon " urged, " The British Constitution is made to Secure Liberty and Property; whatever takes away these, takes away the Constitution itself, and cannot be constitutional." [3]

It is possible, of course, that these letters were written by Americans masquerading as natives of England, but it is certain that such ideas were held by a considerable body of Englishmen. The argument is not often stated so clearly as in the above extracts, but it seems to have been the probable intent of a number of Englishmen who protested against the taxation of America as unconstitutional. Lord Camden expressed this view in a parliamentary speech against the

[1] *L. C.*, May 31, 1774; see *London E. P.*, May 13, 1775.
[2] *P. A.*, Feb. 11, 1775; see *S. J. C.*, April 29, 1775.
[3] *S. J. C.*, Aug. 11, 1770; see *ibid.*, Dec. 22, 1768.

Declaratory Act, and it is well known that others held it.[1]
In 1775 the *London Packet* reported a speech by Mr. Stone
at the Court of Common Council on the doctrine of parliamentary supremacy.   According to the reporter:

> he proved from authentic history, and law books, that parliament
> was inferior to law; that it was instituted to preserve, not to
> abrogate the law: he quoted instances from Bracton down to
> Fortescue, Coke, and Blackstone, to support his opinion, and
> offered to contend it upon constitutional grounds against any
> man, whether of the profession of the law or not! . . . he then
> adapted these arguments to the American contest, and in our
> correspondent's opinion clearly established his point, that parlia-
> ment had no constitutional *right to tax America* INTERNALLY.

The correspondent added that his speech " was received with
every proper mark of approbation."[2]

The doctrine that Parliament is sovereign is of comparatively late development.[3] The American revolutionists had
taken many of their political ideas from an earlier England
when parliamentary sovereignty was not known or was im-
perfectly accepted.   American political ideas were largely
derived from those Puritans, who in the troublesome mid-
seventeenth century, had drawn up a written constitution
as fundamental law to govern England.[4] In America, where
it was less crowded by established systems and interests, this
idea of fundamental constitutional law, to which all other
law must conform, had gained far more acceptance than in
England, where, though it could not dominate, it none the
less lived.[5]

[1] See a discussion in Adams, R. G., *Political Ideas of the American
Revolution* (Trinity College Press, 1922), p. 128; see Haines, *American
Doctrine of Judicial Supremacy* (New York, 1914), pp. 28, 37.

[2] *L. P.*, Feb. 22, 1775.

[3] See Adams, *op. cit.*, p. 126; McIlwain, *High Court of Par.*, preface,
p. ix, p. 60.

[4] McIlwain, *High Court of Par.*, p. 60 *et seq.*, p. 91 *et seq.*

[5] See *Gent. Mag.*, Feb., 1775, p. 71.

"Numa," one of the most prominent administration writers of the later period, sought to enlighten Englishmen on the nature of their constitution. He complained that no word was so frequently used nor so little understood as "constitution," and maintained that the ones who used it most were "eternally endeavouring to subvert it." "By the *Constitution* of this Country, the supreme Power of the State is exclusively lodged with the King, Lords and Commons in Parliament." Having given what had become the orthodox view of the constitution, he turned upon the Patriots and charged that they were the ones who were subverting it.[1] "Numa" raised the wrath of "A. B.," who charged him with designing "to establish the favourite Doctrine of all Tyrants, namely, that the supreme Power of a Nation has Authority to pass what Laws they please, and that the People are guilty of Arrogance, Presumption, and I know not what, if they pretend to interfere with them in any Degree." He would have "Numa" know that "King, Lords and Commons are the Creatures of the People, appointed and paid by them to do their Business; if therefore they either neglect it through Laziness, or betray it through Villainy, have not the People a Right to admonish them of it, and call them to an Account for it?"[2] "One of the Public," a pro-American writer in the *Public Advertiser*, urged that members of Parliament were but the trustees of the people to preserve the constitution, and "whenever under the sanction of Laws, any Thing iniquitous is enacted, it becomes *ipso facto* void; and as Inequity can never be Law, it is lawful to resist such Acts in their Execution."[3] A *Gentleman's Magazine* writer said, "if the Americans contend for anything, and if they know

[1] *P. A.*, May 20, 1775.

[2] *P. A.*, May 29, 1775.

[3] *P. A.*, March 28, 1775; see *London Mag.*, Jan., 1766, p. 33.

what is worth contending for, it is a PERMANENT CONSTI-
TUTION." [1] Although, plainly, a section of the English
public held views as to the nature of their constitution that
were at variance with the generally accepted ideas, views
which put them in sympathy with the claims of their American brethren beyond the seas, those who held to the legal
omnipotence of Parliament had the greater weight of newspaper opinion.

Unfortunately it is usually impossible to determine in
what sense an Englishman of the time used the word " unconstitutional." He may have had the conventional English ideas and have meant only that an act was contrary to
custom; but many another Englishman used the word in the
sense of the modern American, an " unconstitutional " act
being one which was contrary to the principles of a constitution which was higher than Parliament.

What was the English constitution? What rights did it
guarantee? Most commonly it was declared that the bul-
wark of the constitution was " that the people shall not be
taxed but by their own consent." This, it was argued, was
a right no parliament could abrogate. It alone was sufficient
to confirm them in their liberties; to defend it the blood of
a king had been shed. [2] It had been the principle of the resistance to ship money, and American taxation and ship
money were declared to involve the same principle. [3] In this
matter Englishmen were fond of quoting the great philosopher, Locke. [4] A larger view of the constitution was found
in the assertion that " English liberty . . . might be defined,
as the primitive right that every freeholder had of *consenting*

[1] *Gent. Mag.*, Nov., 1775, p. 543.
[2] *L. P.*, April 20, 1774.
[3] *L. P.*, March 22, 1775.
[4] *L. C.*, June 9, 1774.

to those laws by which the community was to be obliged." [1]
Against these principles in the abstract no one objected, but
when they were applied to the concrete colonial situation
opinions began to diverge. English sympathizers with
America declared that neither in the colonies nor in England
could the doctrine of parliamentary sovereignty prevail.

To many an Englishman point was given to his objections to parliamentary sovereignty by the imperfections of
the English parliamentary system.[2]   Rotten boroughs and
the prevailing flood of corruption made it easy to cast re-
flections upon the working of that system. The American
disputes, coming at the same time as the Wilkes incidents,
caused Englishmen to examine their constitution as they
had not had occasion to do for generations. Especially did
the American claim of "no taxation without representation"
cause them to investigate the whole question of representation. What they found at home was unsatisfactory to many
of them, who not infrequently called attention to the fact
that the existence of rotten boroughs made representation
in England sadly inadequate. A paragrapher said it was
proper " that every Englishman should be truly apprized of
the monstrous inequality of our parliamentary system." [3]
" A Plain Dealer " urged that Englishmen were " to the
full as critically situated as the colonists. . . ." Continuing,
he said, " Example has ever been held more powerful than
precept, the Americans, by showing us what they *would*,
teach us what we ought to do." [4]   It is probable that the
searchings instigated by the American troubles hastened the
agitation for parliamentary reform in England. Though
that reform did not take place until 1832, sentiment for it

[1] *L. C.,* Nov. 30, 1765; see *L. P.,* April 20, 1764.

[2] *Gaz.,* April 7, 1774.

[3] *Newcastle Chronicle,* March 12, 1774.

[4] *L. P.,* Aug. 19, 1774; see *P. A.,* April 28, 1775.

had appeared years before 1789, when the French Revolution broke out and delayed change for nearly half a century.

Many, besides deploring the inadequacy of representation in England, scornfully denounced the widespread corruption in the political life of the time. Bribery, vote selling and sale of parliamentary seats were so common as to be almost the rule. Selling of seats was so open that sometimes it was advertised in the public press.[1] A *Middlesex Journal* paragraph lamented the shameful traffic in boroughs, so openly carried on " that printed bills " had been sent " to several of the postmasters on the Norfolk road, advertising two boroughs for *sale.*" [2] " Rationalis " foresaw the downfall of the constitution unless it could be secured against the " extending powers of Corruption." [3] It is recognized to-day that modern English political life has never seen a more venal period than the early years of the reign of George the Third. Englishmen of the time, well aware of the situation, frequently raised their voices to bewail the decline of morals in public life. Many would have agreed with the first six verses of a political poem in the *St. James's Chronicle:*

> " 'Tis said, good Folks, your Constitution's gone,
>   Your three Estates are shrivil'd up to one.
>   Of King, Lords, Commons, heretofore so fam'd,
>   The latter two only for form are nam'd.
>   Your *Chief* declares *all Blackamores are white:*
>   The Lords (o! wond'rous) cry, the Thing is right." [4]

The fact that the British Parliament of the American Revo-

---

[1] See *S. J. C.,* Jan. 6, 1774; *P. A.,* Jan. 21, 22, 25, 1774; *M. J. & E. A.,* Feb. 3, 1774.

[2] *M. J. & E. A.,* Aug. 23, 1774.

[3] *L. C.,* Oct. 1, 1765.

[4] *S. J. C.,* May 2, 1775; see *L. P.,* March 14, 1774; *Univ. Mag.,* Aug., 1772, p. 62.

lutionary period, because corruptly controlled by the king, was by no means so responsive to the will of the people as are modern democratic legislatures, is one that cannot be disregarded when English opinion is under consideration.

In defining representation there was room for honest disagreement between Americans and Englishmen, and between Englishmen of different political faiths. In answer to American cries of "no representation," Englishmen advanced the old English theory of "virtual representation." To Americans and to many Englishmen, virtual representation was a farce, a travesty; yet the Englishman who advanced it had behind him a tradition of long standing. The present-day American theory that a representative should represent his own constituency only, had not been accepted. It was known, however, for "Demophoon" flatly stated, "Every representative in parliament is not a representative for the whole nation, but only for the particular place for which he hath been chosen."[1] According to the accepted English theory, however, a member of the House of Commons from any given part of England represented not only his own constituency, but also all other members of the commonalty within the empire.[2] Thus many Englishmen, when taken to task because of the rotten boroughs in England, and when told that Manchester, Birmingham, Leeds, Sheffield and other great cities were not represented, replied that they were virtually represented, that the commons of these cities were represented by others of their own class from all parts of the kingdom; and would have agreed with "Pacificus" that "The doctrine of virtual representation is the very basis on which our constitution stands."[3]

Hence when sympathizers with America contended that

[1] *S. J. C.,* Aug. 11, 1770; *London Mag.,* Aug., 1770, p. 417.
[2] See *L. C.,* Feb. 18, 1766; *Gaz.,* Feb. 4, 1766.
[3] *Lloyd's E. P.,* Dec. 11, 1765.

taxation of America was wrong because the Americans were not represented, Englishmen answered that they were as much represented as the inhabitants of the above-mentioned cities, and that these citizens had never contended that they were exempt from taxation. " Britophilus " thought the American cry of " no taxation without representation " the most plausible argument they had, but in opposition he wanted to know who were the representatives of every Briton " who has not a freehold of forty shillings? who of the freemen of London not Liverymen? who of the proprietors of copyhold or leasehold estates? "[1] To the earnest conservative believer in things as they were, to those who believed the British constitution the frame of the most perfect government the sun had ever shone upon, it was easy, after showing by English theory that these people were virtually represented, to apply the principle to the colonies, and to declare that they were as much represented as the majority of Englishmen themselves. To those Englishmen who were not satisfied with the rotten borough system and with English representation in general, a justification of the American measures by reference to them was but poor reasoning, since it was simply " one inequality, blemish, anomaly, or imperfection in our constitution, . . . produced as a justification of another."[2] James Otis in his pamphlet, *Considerations on Behalf of the Colonists,* had argued that the great English towns ought to be represented, and the *Monthly Review* commented, " we entirely acquiesce in our Author's laconic reply, ' *That it is high time they should.*' "[3] Another time on the subject of inadequate representation in England, it said, " It is certainly a defect, but we must make

[1] *L. C.,* Dec. 17, 1765.
[2] *L. C.,* March 6, 1766.
[3] *Monthly Rev.,* Nov., 1765, p. 399.

the best of our government as we find it." [1] The colonists' arguments were slowly causing Englishmen to see flaws in their own system.

Some Englishmen, who apparently adopted the virtual-representation theory as applied to England, were quick to point out that there was no comparison when the attempt was made to apply it to the colonies. It was declared that the case of the large English towns was not the same as that of the colonies, for when Parliament voted a tax on the towns, it at the same time voted a tax on itself; but the taxes voted on the colonies were for them only and were not felt at all by the Parliament that imposed them. [2] The cases would be parallel if the Parliament were to impose a separate tax on the towns that did not send members to it, and excuse from taxation those that did. Although virtual representation continued to be urged throughout the period, no single argument used by the anti-American forces seems to have been so well answered. It was refuted by logic, scoffed at, derided, ridiculed, called an " audacious insult," [3] " mere sophistry," " the product of a heated imagination." [4] And yet it would not down; it continued to be advocated until the sword was advanced to settle the dispute.

" H " sought to meet the colonists' cry of " no taxation without representation" by urging that the " TRUE and ONLY constitutional " way of taxing America was to make all laws designed to tax her " become so far general Laws, as to affect England and the Colonies alike; so that no tax " might be paid " for our distant Provinces " but what Englishmen should be obliged " to pay in the Same Manner and

[1] *Ibid.*, April, 1774, p. 272.

[2] *Universal Mag.*, Supp., 1774, p. 363; see March, 1776, p. 144; *S. J. C.*, March 31, 1774 and Jan. 12, 1775; *London Mag.*, Feb., 1768, p. 76.

[3] *Universal Mag.*, May, 1775, p. 234.

[4] *L. C.*, Oct. 31, 1775.

Proportion at home." In the case of the Stamp Act this principle would have meant that the existing stamp tax in England would be repealed, and a new one passed applying to America as well as to England.[1] This suggested solution of the problem, however, gained but little support.

The English newspapers were full of discussion concerning the constitutionality of taxation. Taxation without representation was variously described by writers friendly to America as " the main point," [2] " the primary cause " of the trouble,[3] " the real question in dispute," [4] " the ground of this unhappy contest," [5] " the bitter Root from Whence all these Evils " grew,[6] " the whole dispute; " [7] to it all other matters were " merely collateral." [8] In England as in America the slogan "No Taxation without Representation" might have been a watchword of liberty.

The difference in principle, or lack of difference, between internal and external taxes was one of the issues, especially in the early part of the dispute. Grenville and Pitt in the House of Commons had taken opposite sides on the question, Pitt thinking the principle involved was not the same. Franklin, when examined before the House of Commons, January 28, 1766, thought likewise. If there was not a genuine difference in principle there was at least a distinction. On the whole the newspaper opinion was that the difference, if any, was slight. " Benevolus " was willing to grant that perhaps the alleged difference was " groundless

[1] *P. L.*, May 7, 1774; see *M. C.*, April 6, 1774 and Feb. 12, 1774.

[2] *L. C.*, Nov. 2, 1775.

[3] *L. C.*, Feb. 11, 1775.

[4] *Gent. Mag.*, Feb., 1775, p. 69.

[5] *L. C.*, Nov. 4, 1775.

[6] *S. J. C.*, Dec. 24, 1772.

[7] *Universal Mag.*, Sept., 1768, p. 121.

[8] *L. P.*, March 30, 1774.

and frivolous," and that external and internal taxes were the same. If that was true, as most asserted, then he charged that the onus was on those who persisted in imposing internal taxes on the Americans. The colonists were making no objections to external taxation in the early years of the controversy, and as Englishmen were asserting it was the same as internal taxation, why bother to irritate them when as much money as England ought to expect could be drawn in less irritating ways?[1]

Some argued that the Americans had already accepted taxation, and internal taxation at that, for, so these said, the whole post-office system in America was internal and required the payment of internal duties.[2] The argument, though not often advanced, to logical, legal minds provided a precedent; and of logic the advocates of strong action against the Americans were always fond.[3] When the post-office argument was used it almost always elicited an answer from some friend to America who pointed out that the post-office rules could be considered properly only " as regulations of convenience " established for the convenience of both countries, and that postal charges were not a tax inasmuch as they extracted not a farthing from those who did not voluntarily use the postal system.[4]

In December, 1765, the printers, noticing that the Americans were pleading " their charters against complying with the stamp act," began to print extracts from the several charters that it might be seen by all " on what foundation "

[1] L. C., April 7, 1767; see Jan. 31, 1775.

[2] Lloyd's E. P., Jan. 24, 1766; P. A., Jan. 11, 1770.

[3] In reading Tory arguments one is often reminded of a contemporary criticism, " Metaphysical refinements in philosophy, as well as politics, have given rise to many questions which common sense rejects." L. C., March 27, 1766.

[4] Lloyd's E. P., Jan. 27, 1766; see Gaz., Feb. 3, 1766.

they conducted themselves.[1]   During the month extracts from the charters of nearly every colony were printed. The parts most generally selected for publication were those which granted to the colonists all the rights of Englishmen " born within the Realm of England." The Pennsylvania charter alone was quoted as clearly showing that Parliament had a right to tax a colony.[2] In dealing with the other charters, the disputants on both sides contented themselves with implications or intent.

The friends of America who used the charter arguments relied especially upon those sections which granted to colonists all the rights of Englishmen born within the realm. According to them, high among the most precious of English rights was that of being taxed by their own representatives. Denying, as they did, that the Americans were represented, they insisted that American taxation was in violation of this clause of their charters. The believers in virtual representation simply used that theory to prove that their rights as Englishmen were not being violated when they were subjected to taxation, but to believers in the sovereignty of Parliament there was an answer more conclusive.

This latter group simply asserted that Parliament was sovereign and could alter all charters at will. Those of this persuasion wrote to the papers in agreement with the paragraph, "The people of Boston lay great stress on their charters derived from the Crown, as if a British Parliament had not a legal right to annul all charters prejudicial to the interests of England."[3]   " Opifex," and Jo. Wheeler of Ulverstone, and " T. N.," the latter writing from the

---

[1] *London Mag.*, Appendix, 1765, p. 674.

[2] They printed the section which granted to Penn and his heirs all customs and subsidies " saving unto Us, Our Heirs and Successors, such Impositions and Customs, as by Act of Parliament are and shall be appointed." *S. J. C.*, Dec. 17, 1765; *M. J. & E. A.*, Aug. 27, 1774.

[3] *K. G.*, Sept. 8, 1772.

Temple, were prominent asserters of this argument.[1] As in all the arguments of the pen, few seem to have been convinced, for the debate was still raging at the end of the pre-revolutionary period. A favorite pro-American argument was that all " Rights, Privileges &c. which British Subjects now enjoy" had been obtained from kings by stipulations, agreements and compacts, which was the method by which the Americans got their charters.[2] If the kings granted such rights to their subjects in England, why could they not do the same in America? The colonial charters were compared to Magna Carta and it was declared that Parliament could as well annihilate its provisions as tax the colonists contrary to their charters.[3]

In the final analysis the chief argument used by newspaper writers against the Americans was based on this claim of parliamentary sovereignty. " J. P. S. L. H." saw to the heart of the question, and praised Lord North for stripping it to its simplest statement in maintaining " that the whole reasoning on this question may be fairly deduced from one single postulate, viz. that the Inhabitants of the British Colonies are Subjects of the British State." [4] To the logical conservative mind the whole case was settled by such a statement. All subjects must pay taxes. That seemed easy to understand. If the Americans were subjects, then they must pay taxes imposed by the supreme power of the state, which was Parliament. The Americans were plainly subjects. Therefore they must pay. No problem in geometry, thought some newspaper writers, could be clearer than that. The whole matter hinged there and was settled there. What

---

[1] See *L. C.*, May 10, 1774; *S. J. C.*, Jan. 21, 1775 and *L. C.*, March 19, 1774 respectively.

[2] *S. J. C.*, Oct. 29, 1774.

[3] *S. J. C.*, Oct. 29, 1774.

[4] *L. C.*, June 4, 1774; see *L. C.*, March 6, 1766, Dec. 1, 1774.

more conclusive proof of the right of American taxation could any one desire? If that one point were once established all other arguments would be unnecessary; useful and not to be abandoned, but to be maintained merely as secondary defences.

If the conservatives expected their opponents quietly to accept this doctrine and argue no more they were quickly disappointed. No one denied that the Americans were British subjects, but many denied that all such subjects paid taxes imposed by the British Parliament. It was early pointed out that although the Irish were likewise subjects, Parliament did not see fit to impose internal taxes on them. The Isle of Man, the Isles of Guernsey [1] and Jersey, Wales, Chester, Durham and Convocation of the Clergy were all cited to prove that there were or had been subjects who had not been taxed by Parliament.

The precedent of Ireland was the favorite one advanced. Early in 1766 the *London Magazine* printed some remarks of Blackstone to the effect that taxation of the colonies was legal. At the end of the article the printer, with the air of one who had not been convinced, wished he could have Blackstone's opinion upon the reputed old statute *De Tallagio non concedendo* on which seemed to be founded the reason why Ireland, the Isle of Man, Jersey and Guernsey had never been taxed.[2] The writer of a set of queries wanted to know if the Irish " as a subordinate people " had any constitutional rights to which the Americans were not entitled.[3] America was asserted to have an even better case than Ireland, because the latter was a conquered country.[4] " Paci-

---

[1] For a discussion of Guernsey see William Berry, *History of the Island of Guernsey* (London, 1815), p. 220 *et seq.*

[2] *London Mag.*, Jan., 1766, p. 3.

[3] *L. C.*, Feb. 1, 1766.

[4] *P. A.*, Jan. 8, 1770.

ficus " demanded to know what difference there was in the status of the two parts of the empire.[1]

Ireland could not be taxed, it was alleged, because she had no representation in the British Parliament and because she had a parliament of her own. The colonies were asserted to be in the same case. A *London Chronicle* writer challenged all politicians, including Mansfield and North, to resist two reputed statutes passed, " the 8th of Richard II. ch. 12. and the 20th of Henry VI. Chapter 8." in which it was stated that:

' a tax granted by the Parliament of England shall *not* bind those of Ireland, *because* they are not summoned to our Parliament; that Ireland hath a Parliament of its own, and maketh and altereth laws; and our statutes do *not* bind them, but their *persons* are the King's *subjects,* like as the inhabitants of Calais, Gascoigny and Guienne.' [2]

The contributor of a set of pertinent quotations in the *St. James's Chronicle* called attention to these two declarations but indicated that they were not statutes but were opinions of judges of the respective monarchs.[3]

Less frequently than to the Irish precedent, attention was called to the fact that other subjects had been exempt from parliamentary taxation either because of charter grants or because they had a representative body which imposed their own taxation. Chester and Durham were cases that might be cited by either side; they had both been taxed despite the facts that they had no representation in Parliament and that they had representative bodies of their own. But the friends

[1] *S. J. C.,* March 31, 1774.

[2] *L. C.,* April 19, 1774; also in *Gaz.,* April 18, 1774.

[3] *S. J. C.,* Jan. 14, 1775; for other references to the Irish precedent see *S. J. C.,* Jan. 4, 1766, Aug. 11, 1770, March 31, April 30, May 21, Dec. 8, 1774; *Gaz.,* Jan. 3, 1766, March 31, 1774; *M. C.,* Feb. 22, 1775; *L. C.,* June 9, 1774, Nov. 14, 1775.

of America were able to point out that such taxation had been objected to at the time as irregular, and had been dropped.[1] "Aratus" called attention to the fact that early English kings had not taxed the clergy without first consulting their representatives in convocation assembled.[2]

The advocates of American taxation never met these precedents squarely. Sometimes they alleged that Ireland had been taxed, but they never claimed that it had been done habitually. To explain this failure they asserted that the Irish themselves had made due contributions, thus sparing England the trouble of collecting taxes, which she would certainly have done if the Irish had not contributed.[3] "Unison" attempted to explain the matter by saying that the Irish were thus favored because, when they gave up a government of their own, the English had made them some concessions. But the colonists had never, in the same sense, had their own governments, so there was no need to make concessions to them.[4] "Mentor," writer of many anti-American letters, after arguing that the Americans, being subjects, must pay, peevishly took notice of allusions to Ireland, saying, "I bar all references to Ireland," giving as reason the fact that England had no dispute with Ireland. By simply barring references he thought to get rid of a troublesome question. All remarks concerning Ireland he classed as "wicked subterfuges."[5] Most writers on his side either barred Ireland or simply disregarded it. They may have had good arguments to show that the Irish and the American cases were not parallel in respect to taxation, but

[1] See *L. C.,* March 26, 1768; *London Mag.,* May, 1776, p. 253; *S. J. C.* Feb. 7, 1775.

[2] *L. C.,* June 9, 1774.

[3] *L. P.,* Feb. 3, 1775.

[4] *P. A.,* Jan. 1, 1768.

[5] *P. A.,* Oct. 14, 1768.

if they did they were never successful in giving them extended newspaper publicity.

The friends of the colonists sometimes insisted that American taxation was unconstitutional, and that the Americans were right in giving resistance because they were defending privileges that were theirs " from long quiet possession or what is called *prescription.*" [1] " Every former parliament before 1764," [2] it was alleged, had left them undisturbed in internal taxation, and there were many who thought that as internal taxation had been waived for one hundred years past it might safely be waived for the century to come.[3] If England would treat the colonies as they had been treated before the late peace, all trouble would be allayed. Go back to 1760, cried some, and do unto them as they were done unto then.[4] That this argument was not prominent in the press is perhaps the reason why few attempts at rebuttal were made, but it is difficult to see how rebuttals could have been successful.

Another argument, dealt with more fully in the next chapter, was that taxation of the colonies was unconstitutional because America, by right, was exempt not merely from laws of taxation, but from all parliamentary law.

[1] *L. C.,* Nov. 12, 1768; see Oct. 20, 1768.

[2] *P. A.,* Feb. 6, 1775.

[3] *L. C.,* Nov. 2, 1775.

[4] *K. G.,* Oct. 11, 1775; *L. P.,* April 1, 1774; *S. J. C.,* Aug. 24, 1775.

CHAPTER V

COLONIAL AND IMPERIAL THINKING

MOST Englishmen who took up the pen against the Americans thought of the settlements beyond the seas as " our colonies," " our possessions "; and of the colonists as " our subjects." The colonies were, to be sure, a part of the empire, but a part owned by England, not in any sense an extension of England; valuable not as Cornwall or Yorkshire were valuable, but only as they brought in some very tangible profit to the home country. When they thought of America they thought of benefits to England. If a slogan had been used it would have been " America for Englishmen," not " America for Americans." Rob. Richardson, writing in the *London Chronicle,* expressed a common opinion when he declared, "The colonies were acquired with no other view than to be a convenience to us; and therefore it can never be imagined that we are to consult their interests preferably to our own." [1] " Britannicus " plainly told the public that the Americans were " not their fellow-citizens, but their subjects. . . ." [2]

It is of small use to criticize the Englishmen of that day for this way of thinking, for they were still living under the spell of the mercantile theory, a theory which taught subordination of every means to the great end of national strength against all rivals. They lived under the teachings of the old colonial system which taught that colonies were valuable for what they could contribute. In addition, their

[1] *L. C.,* July 31, 1764; see *M. C.,* March 27, April 4, 1775.
[2] *P. A.,* Jan. 25, 1775.

thinking had not kept pace with the developments of the years. Their thoughts were often more appropriate to the America of 1670 than to that of 1770. Their children beyond the seas were growing up; they were getting beyond the apron-string stage; yet many Englishmen thought of them as in swaddling clothes. Such thinking ill fitted Englishmen for conciliation where America was concerned.

America, thought many in 1770 must pay taxes; if she did not, of what value was she? They sometimes went even further, by declaring that if the colonists did not contribute taxes, England was subservient, for in that case she carried much more than her just proportion of the load of empire. If Americans continued to escape taxation while being protected by the British army and navy, then their brethren in England "burdened with taxes" were "hewers of wood and drawers of water for them. . . ."[1] The mental attitude of the present-day Englishmen who take comfort in thinking of Canada or of Australia as a part of the empire, with never a thought of securing taxes or other tribute from them, would have been incomprehensible to their ancestors of 1770, for the modern English attitude toward colonies had not been born.

Administration supporters were also prone to assume that the colonies and all that they represented were a monument to government action. According to their theory the colonies were founded by such action; they were nursed in their infancy by it; they were protected and helped at every stage by government. These advocates seemed to ignore all other theories as to the colonies, and exhibited an extreme belief, that, without the solicitude of a maternal and self-sacrificing government, nothing in America would have been.[2]

[1] *L. C.*, Oct. 31, 1775; see *L. C.*, Nov. 24, April 21, 1774; *S. J. C.*, Aug. 21, 1775; *Lloyd's E. P.*, April 11, 1774; Feb. 7, 1770.

[2] See *Gaz.*, April 13, 1767.

"Britannicus," in giving his ideas on colonies, admirably stated the thought of many a letter writer when he said:

I have always considered the Colonies as the great *farms* of the public, and the Colonists as our tenants, whom I wish to have treated kindly whilst they act as such; but when they usurp the inheritance, and tell us they are and will be independent of us, it is time to look about us, and keep them to the *terms* of their leases; but they seem to think every degree of subjection is slavery. . . . [1]

Is it strange "Atraea" asserted that many had "looked upon the American Colonists as little more than a Set of Slaves, at work for us, in distant Plantations, one Degree only above the Negroes, that, we carry to them." [2] "S." used the language of parable. Nothing, he thought, could be more plain than that the Americans owed "subjection and tribute" to the mother country that had brought them up. But, he complained, the Americans worked evil, for when those who had planted the vineyard, hedged it and let it out that the husbandmen should give of the fruits, lo, they "killed some, tar and feathered others, . . . and . . . say, the inheritance shall be their own. . . ." [3]

"Prestoniesis" was sure that a colony should have no arts that could rival those of the mother country for "a Colony, incapable of producing any other commodities than those produced by its Mother Country, would be more dangerous than useful; it would be proper to call home its Inhabitants and give it up." Colonies were designed for agriculture only. "This maxim," he said, "cannot be contested." [4] "A Manufacturer" thought colonizing could be

[1] *L. P.*, Jan. 4, 1775.
[2] *S. J. C.*, Nov. 16, 1769.
[3] *L. C.*, Aug. 29, 1775.
[4] *S. J. C.*, Feb. 23, 1769.

justified only if it should " add to the wealth and power of the state. If a new settlement " was peopled " from the Mother Country, the latter " became the weaker by the loss of emigrants, and its finances were reduced " in proportion " to the number who emigrated if they were not taxed in the new colony.[1] " Rationalis " was certain the great object in regard to North America was that of " vending our manufactures," [2] and "Philanthropus" had the same idea.[3] These last two writers belonged to a school that was quite willing to waive taxation, for the same results, they thought, could be secured in another way.

" Creon," in a letter of more than usual significance, for the printer appended a note saying that his letters were inspired by the administration and " seemed written to feel the pulse of the public," baldly stated that " subjects ought to lose some of their privileges by migration." If this was not done the empire would be no longer an empire but only a confederacy. The Americans had been granted too much liberty; some of it must be taken from them; and never was the time more propitious than the present.[4]

Englishmen with the views that have just been mentioned were fond of employing the mother and child argument. The first settlers were children of Great Britain, protected by her, and for them the home country had " exhausted her strength like an affectionate mother ";[5] her blood and treasure had been poured out for her offspring; in fact, America had been so tenderly treated that she had become a spoiled child.[6] Especially, as we have noted in discussing the Stamp

[1] *L. C.,* Dec. 8, 1774.
[2] *Gent. Mag.,* Nov., 1765, p. 573; see *Univ. Mag.,* March, 1774.
[3] *Lloyd's E. P.,* April 17, 1772.
[4] *Lloyd's E. P.,* May 11, 1770.
[5] *L. C.,* Nov. 25, 1773.
[6] *L. C.,* June 24, 1775.

Act period, did they dwell upon the millions expended in the late war, a war begun, so they said, at the earnest entreaty of the colonies, entered into " solely in their Defence." [1]

Increasingly as the American problem became a knotty one for British statesmen, a note of bitterness crept into the discussions. This was seen, for example, in questionings as to the value of colonies, whether they were not on the whole injurious rather than beneficial. The idea that colonies were harmful to the mother country was not new, but it received encouragement from the refractory conduct overseas. During the Stamp Act period, "Cattshill" questioned the value of colonies, asserting that their late conduct must have caused many other Englishmen to think likewise. It is neither wise nor prudent, he wrote, for an island nation, whose chief strength is in ships and sailors, to plant a continental colony, for as such a one grows it will begin to assert its independence and, since the home country will be unable to reduce it to obedience, it will at last become a rival. This condition, he thought, had been reached in America: the Americans, recently freed by the victory over the French, from all enemies except a few Indians, now felt themselves strong enough to throw off all subjection. If they were only island colonies, their subjection would be an easy thing, but continental colonies were a different matter. [2]

The idea that the fear of French encroachment was the chief tie holding the colonies to England, a tie which would vanish with the disappearance of the fear, had long been known; [3] and newspaper comment showed that it had some acceptance. " Cattshill," [4] "An European " [5] and numerous

---

[1] *S. J. C.,* Dec. 22, 1774; *L. C.,* Dec. 3, 1774.

[2] *S. J. C.,* Jan. 25, 1766; see *Gaz.,* Feb. 12, 1766.

[3] See Howard, *op. cit.,* pp. 7-8.

[4] *S. J. C.,* Jan. 25, 1766.

[5] *L. C.,* Oct. 13, 1768.

paragraphers agreed with " B. C." that a prime cause of the American troubles was the fact that the English had " taken the French off their backs and placed them in a state of security." [1] Indeed, one paragrapher reported rumors "that a Negotiation is on the Tapis for restoring Canada to France, in return for one of their Sugar Islands, as the most effectual means of securing the Dependence of America on the Mother Country." [2]

Choiseul, the famous French statesman, was quoted to the effect that he had ceded Canada to England on purpose to destroy her, the colonies with this addition becoming so large that they would drain England of her inhabitants and become a rival that would cause her ruin. Commentators on Choiseul, beginning to doubt the value of colonies, thought his words prophetic. [3] One bitter humorist wanted to sell the colonies; he apportioned them out, this one to France, another to the Grand Turk, still another to the Dey of Algiers, " and if his Infernal Highness the Devil would continue to exercise his Sovereign Power over the Bostonian Saints, *to let him have them on his own terms.*" Boston had long since been singled out as the ringleader. An opposition paragrapher, however, took note of the opinion that colonists were loads and burdens, charging that a late administration had propagated such ideas at a time when " they had drawn themselves into a very disagreeable contest with them," a contest from which they did not know the way out. [4] The grapes were getting a little sour.

The mercantile attitude toward colonies is also shown by

[1] *L. C.,* Sept. 17, 1774; see *M. P.,* Feb. 18, 1774; *M. J. & E. A.,* Feb. 8, 1774.

[2] *P. A.,* Nov. 7, 1768.

[3] *K. G.,* Oct. 24, 1772; see *G. E. P.* and *L. C.,* July 13, 1775.

[4] *M. J. & E. A.,* Nov. 1, 1774; see *S. J. C.,* Jan. 25, 1766; *L. C.,* Oct. 5, 1773, Oct. 31, 1775; *L. P.,* Feb. 3, 1775; *K. G.,* July 21, 1772.

a very common feeling of jealousy toward the Americans, a feeling that they were rivals to be watched, to be kept down. This was shown especially in the attitude of those solicitous for British manufactures, who on the immediate question of taxation or harsh measures against the Americans were usually to be classed as pro-American, and for this reason : The colonies, if irritated too much, would begin to manufacture for themselves, and thus destroy their worth to England, for according to mercantile ideas if a colony's products competed with home products, the colony's value was lessened to the extent of that competition.[1]   Those jealous of America also wanted to keep the Americans divided as much as possible in feeling, for then only could England manage them.[2]

The English were well aware of the rapid increase of American population. They knew Franklin's estimate which doubled "the American Population every twenty-five years," and to some this was a matter of concern.[3]   One querist asked how long it would be before the Americans, whom he estimated at three millions, would be doubled in numbers. "And then how are we to rule them?"[4]   A *Public Advertiser* paragraph stated, " It appears according to the Laws of Population, the Number of white Inhabitants in our several American Colonies, will in one Century more be increased to 22 Millions and a half."   Then it added, " Is not this an alarming Circumstance?"[5]   A humorous skit pictured two Americans on a visit to London in 1974, finding it in ruins as Balbec, Persepolis, Athens and Rome. Britain, largely because of her injustice to America, had declined,

[1] S. J. C., Feb. 21, 1769.

[2] *London Mag.*, Jan., 1771, p. 24; M. J. & E. A., Aug. 25, 1774.

[3] P. A., Oct. 21, 1771; see *Lloyd's E. P.*, Dec. 18, 1769.

[4] L. C., Feb. 1, 1766; see L. C., March 23, 1765.

[5] P. A., Dec. 7, 1768; see S. J. C., April 6, 1775.

and the colonies had become the seat of empire.[1] A contributor sending in Bishop Berkeley's famous poem, the last stanza of which begins, " Westward the course of Empire takes its way," wondered if the prophecy were true.[2] Another thought New York might " be to London what Byzantium was to Rome." [3] " Britannicus " was surprised that the idea of America as the future seat of empire found " so general a reception among us," and denounced it as absurd; [4] but absurd or not it was common, and the picture of a great, flourishing, strong civilization on the far side of the Atlantic was one which enemies of American claims viewed with jealous misgivings and which friends held up as a reason why conciliating measures should be adopted.

Emigration was frequently a topic of interest to the printers.[5] England was advised not to encourage the population of the colonies either from England itself or from foreign countries, because it was " pernicious to ourselves." [6] The favorite word applied to emigration was "alarming." Sometimes this was because it drained England of valuable inhabitants, for the strength of a nation was commonly al-

[1] *Lloyd's E. P.*, Nov. 28, 1774.

[2] *Chester Chronicle*, Oct. 30, 1775.

[3] *Gaz.*, Oct. 17, 1767.

[4] *M. J. & E. A.*, March 1, 1774; see *London Mag.*, Jan., 1771, p. 24, Aug., 1768, p. 430; *Univ. Mag.*, Supp., 1774, p. 363; *Gent. Mag.*, Feb., 1775, p. 70; *K. G.*, March 26, 1774; *L. P.*, June 6, Nov. 23, 1774; *G. E. P.*, June 4, 1774.

[5] See *K. G.*, May 16, 1772; *Univ. Mag.*, Jan., 1774, p. 51; *Lloyd's E. P.*, April 8, May 13, Aug. 28, 1772. An interesting letter from Inverness analyzes the reason for the alarming emigrations. Five reasons are economic. The sixth and last is, " There are no titled proud Lords to tyrannize over the lower Sort of People, Men being there upon a Level, and more valued, in Proportion to their Abilities, than they are in Scotland." Given in *S. J. C.*, Jan. 13, 1774; *Univ. Mag.*, Jan., 1774, p. 51; *M. J. & E. A.*, Jan. 13, 1774; *M. P.*, Jan. 12, 1774.

[6] *Lloyd's E. P.*, Sept. 26, 1766; see April 8, May 13, Aug. 28, 1772.

lowed to consist in the number of its people;[1] but often the alarming part of it was that the colonies were already as well stocked as it was " convenient they should be," [2] for if the flow of emigrants to them was not stopped it would prove "destructive to the British Empire." [3]   "A Manufacturer " thought the drain of artificers and manufacturers of all sorts should be added to the other " disadvantages which Great Britain sustains by her American colonies." [4] This is not surprising in a country which had a law making it a capital offence to inveigle artificers and mechanics to leave the kingdom, a law that was, however, as Dean Tucker lamented, " unhappily superseded at present." [5]   Rarely did any writers encourage emigration, and the few who did acknowledged that they were going directly against the accepted opinion.[6]

It is evident, then, that though Englishmen regarded the colonies as part of the Empire, they were for the most part ready to receive them only as inferiors.   Though they were ever proclaiming that the Empire was a unit with no distinctions in the power of parliamentary law in any part, many of them, at the same time, looked upon the colonies as rivals to be subordinated; otherwise, they would become dangerous to England.   In subjection to parliamentary law and the burdens of Empire the Americans were to be equal; in the privileges of Empire they were not to be equal.   To such an attitude, a proud and growing people could best respond by a desire for true equality, and finding that de-

---

[1] *M. C.,* Feb. 11, 1775; *Adam's Weekly Courant,* April 1, 1766.

[2] *K. G.,* Oct. 9, 1773.

[3] *L. C.,* Oct. 5, 1773; see *P. L.,* Sept. 24, 1773.

[4] *L. C.,* Nov. 24, 1774; see *M. J. & E. A.,* Jan. 27, 1774.

[5] *Univ. Mag.,* Feb., 1774, p. 86; see *London E. P.,* July 20, 1765.

[6] See *Gaz.,* Jan. 28, 1768, Jan. 18, 1774; see letter by " Philocles " Aug. 23, 1769 *passim.*

nied, a desire for independence. A stubborn English conservative, logical though he might claim to be, seemed unable to appreciate that America would feel resentment when regarded as a rival and treated with jealousy; he seemed unable to see the disparity between this equality in burdens and inequality in privileges. The Americans themselves thought little of the difference until embittered by years of dissensions.

Not all Englishmen were so blind. One, for example, wrote, "The Americans, however ignorance may believe, or tyranny misrepresent, are much rather the voluntary allies than the dependents of Great Britain." [1] A writer signing himself "An American," who may or may not have had the right to that signature, argued that such partial laws as the Sugar Act were dictated by a narrow mind. He had a truly imperial outlook, and wanted no part to be favored at the expense of any other part: for if the colonies acquired "Riches and Strength," it was the "Riches and Strength of the Community," and to him it seemed "immaterial in what Part of the Empire that Strength" resided. [2] "Raleigh," in an open letter addressed to the Earl of Dartmouth, asserted, "We are jealous of America." In English imagination "America is to be our Rival." He warned against such a feeling, saying he was "confident no such Idea" existed in the colonies but he would "not answer for the consequences which improper Usage on our Part" might produce. Providence had ordained a great increase of wealth and population in America; hence any attempt to stop such increase was both useless and wicked. America was moved "by the finger of God." Soon she would outnumber the population of Great Britain, and then only a policy of mutual interests and affection could keep her at-

[1] *L. P.*, Aug. 31, 1774.
[2] *S. J. C.*, April 18, 1765.

tached to the mother country. United, as they should be, the two could defy the world in arms.[1]

Some pointed out that the colonies had been planted by oppression rather than by maternal care; that conditions in England, whence they fled, had been so bad that if America had not been a vacant land ready to receive them, they would have sought a foreign shore where they would have become a real menace to England; that the Americans had built up a strong civilization in the wilderness, a civilization that brought strength and power to the mother country. The emigration thence had not weakened England, it was asserted, for the " wealth, and potency of the mother country," had been considerably more advanced " than if they had remained in it." [2] Many of the most ardent advocates of harsh measures against the Americans tacitly recognized the same argument when they insisted that America must be brought to terms or England would be ruined. While a few thought it would be better if the colonies were cut adrift, the great bulk of the writers held that such action would mean the end of the power and dominion of England. If the colonies were to become independent, or virtually so, " which God, in pity to this country, forbid . . . ," [3] then, England, they thought, would be ruined, because the existence of all English trade to America was " inseparably connected with the supremacy of Parliament." [4]

Especially well riddled was the argument that England's actions toward America had ever been dictated by altruistic motives. " Americanus " was impatient of the allegation of altruism wherever it was found; entirely too much declamation, he said, had been used on it:

[1] S. J. C., Dec. 24, 1772.
[2] Gent. Mag., Dec., 1765.
[3] G. E. P., Aug. 12, 1775.
[4] L. C., Jan. 12, 1775.

The English speak of the Blood and Treasure they have expended. The Americans, that they have encountered an inhospitable Climate, for the purposes of Great-Britain, and have dedicated their Lives and Fortunes to her Service. There is no Weight in any of these *Declamations*. Whatever was done by either of them, was done for their own Advantage.

They owed each other nothing but mutual affection.[1] Several took pains to assert that the help England had extended to America was not gratuitous; to assert that it was, declared one, was an insult to intelligence. " Is it," asked " The Colonist's Advocate," " Generosity that prompts the Rustick to feed his Cow, which yields him Milk? Could we have been enriched by our Colonies, if we had not defended them from the common Enemy?" [2] "A Reader " could not agree that the expense England had incurred in America was gratuitous " or undergone for any other purpose as much as the interest of England." [3] " B. B.," referring to the claims of altruism many Englishmen made in respect to the late war, asked, " Pray where was it we defended ourselves, or who but our own enemies did we overcome in any part of the globe?" He pointed out the services the colonists themselves had rendered during the conflict.[4] " Spectator " thought the debt England had incurred was great, but against it he would balance all the manifest advantages gained by the war.[5] Paragraphers pointed out that America had done so much during the conflict, that Par-

[1] *S. J. C.*, Dec. 30, 1769. This afterwards appeared in a pamphlet *The Case of Great Britain and America* (London, Phila. reprint, 1789) ; see R. G. Adams, *Pol. Ideas of the Am. Rev.*, p. 13.

[2] *P. A.*, Jan. 29, 1770; see *L. C.*, April 11, 1767; see three American fables, *P. A.*, Jan. 2, 1770.

[3] *Lloyd's E. P.*, April 1, 1774.

[4] *L. C.*, Aug. 22, 1775; see *L. P.*, March 14, 1774.

[5] *S. J. C.*, May 2, 1775; see *K. G.*, May 6, 1775.

liament had seen fit to reimburse them to the extent of £570,000.[1] Others declared that Canada in the hands of the French would have made the French superior in power.[2] There were thus many to declare that England had been moved by no other motive than a regard for English interests and English welfare.

There were some interesting exceptions to the prevailing theories of the value and place of colonies. Adam Smith, whose great book, *The Wealth of Nations*, was published in 1776, was not the only one who was questioning accepted colonial and economic theories. Some agreed with a widely quoted opinion by Lord Kames that the navigation acts were both unjust and impolitic.[3] "Coriolanus" thought them "extremely absurd as well as prejudicial" both to the colonies and to the mother country.[4] Numerous writers were beginning to realize the evils of many mercantile practices and to doubt the value of the time-honored colonial system.

The most widely known and most interesting divergence from the accepted path of colonial thinking was made by Dean Tucker of Gloucester. This worthy churchman could by no means be called a friend of the colonies, but he had ideas concerning them completely at variance with those of most advocates of strong American measures. Although a clergyman by profession, he was an economist by choice and was recognized as one of the foremost authorities on trade in the empire. According to Lecky, the views of Adam Smith were "not very different from those of Tucker."[5] Tucker's ideas were set forth chiefly in two pamphlets: one, published in 1774, dealing with the conduct of the Amer-

---

[1] *K. G.*, Aug. 16 and Sept. 6, 1775.

[2] *S. J. C.*, Aug. 15, 1775; see *K. G.*, April 20, 1774; *L. P.*, Dec. 26, 1774.

[3] *London Mag.*, Nov., 1774, p. 543; *L. C.*, Dec. 13, 1774.

[4] *M. J. & E. A.*, July 5, 1774.

[5] Lecky, *History of England*, vol. iii, p. 389.

icans and the best method of making the colonies useful to
Great Britain; and the other, published in 1775, examining
and comparing the arguments used by Great Britain and her
daughters. His best-known argument setting forth the policy
to follow in regard to the colonies was stated in the first
pamphlet. He discussed five methods of procedure that
might be followed.[1] First, England might muddle along as
she had been doing. Second, the colonists might send
representatives to the British Parliament. Third, they might
be declared rebels and subdued by force of arms. Fourth,
the seat of empire might be bodily transferred to America,
and England might be governed by viceroys. All these
methods he rejected as impossible.

His last method was the one he thought should be followed. It was to separate entirely from the colonies, declare them a free and independent people, and then offer to
guarantee their freedom and independence against all foreign invaders. This revolutionary plan, he asserted, was for
the best interests of both countries. In a very able argument
he denied that such a plan would be tantamount to losing all
benefit from the colonies, and declared that it would make
them more valuable to England than before. Especially
was he explicit in declaring that such a plan would not injure
the trade and shipping of England. To us, one hundred and
fifty years after the event, his arguments seem unanswer-
able. He was driven to his position by a mind of cold logic.
The view of the impartial bystander, he said, was, " If there
be no medium between Dependence and Independence, between Usurpation and a lawful Authority, it necessarily
follows, that your differences can never be reconciled or ad-
justed." [2] Like other devotees of logic in the colonial dis-

[1] What purports to be a sixth method is found in the *London Evening
Post*, July 14, 1774.
[2] See *Univ. Mag.*, Feb., 1775, p. 84.

putes, he could see no gradations, no shadings off; but the
conclusions he arrived at were not the same as those reached
by most.

A theory so much at variance with accepted beliefs might
perhaps be dismissed as the distorted brain fancy of some
impractical visionary; indeed Lecky says it was "then
deemed visionary and almost childish." [1]   But both Dean
Tucker's reputation and the press remarks on it call for
consideration.   The latter show that his ideas were well
known and met with considerable approval.   By some they
were considered "visionary theories," [2] but not by all.   In
1768 "Philo-Britanniae," an anti-American partisan, argued
that the best thing to do was to cut America off, but it appears this step was looked upon by him more as a dreadful
necessity than as a benefit, for it was to be done "as an
unhappy Parent would with a disobedient Child, who had
well nigh ruined him." [3]   The *Monthly Review* said of
Tucker's proposal, "this, however, is not a new idea."   It
had frequently occurred to others "who are daily convinced . . . that we can neither *govern* the Americans, nor
be *governed by them;* that we can neither *unite* with them,
nor ought to think of *subduing* them, and . . . that nothing
remains but to part with them on as friendly terms as we
can." [4]   Though the *Monthly Review* did not approve of
the idea in so many words, the tone of its comment was
favorable.

Paragraphers stated that leaders in administration thought
highly of the idea; they told of the savings in military ex-
penditures, and in bounties that would no longer need to be

[1] Lecky, *op. cit.,* vol. iii, p. 388.

[2] *M. J. & E. A.,* Aug. 25, 1774.

[3] *P. A.,* Sept. 15, 1768.

[4] *Monthly Rev.,* Feb., 1774, pp. 135-136.

paid.[1] One writer in the *St. James's Chronicle* thought no plan seemed to be " more generally approved of than Dr. Tucker's scheme ";[2] another in the *Middlesex Journal and Evening Advertiser* declared, " The soundest politicians are of opinion, that Dean Tucker's advice . . . . is the wisest scheme ever yet proposed for accommodating the present differences, and even strengthening the Mother Country."[3] A correspondent to the *St. James's Chronicle* wrote that he had seen no successful answer to the Dean, and that the errors of the Americans tended " only, at the worst, to dismember an overgrown Empire," which there was " Reason to hope would be more flourishing in Consequence of such an Event."[4] "A Frankelein " was sure the best method to pursue was to separate the whole continent of North America from Great Britain. " Every commercial advantage to both countries may be much better secured by treaty," he thought, " under such separation, than by dragooning the colonists into subjection."[5] Though Tucker cannot be said to have had a wide following, yet such statements as those given above indicate that his ideas fell on a soil that was not entirely unprepared.

John Cartwright also wanted England to declare the independency of America; but by independence he did not mean, as did Tucker, a complete separation from England, but only independence from the Parliament of England, still leaving America under the Crown. His ideas are best known from his pamphlet, *American Independence the Interest and Glory of Great Britain*, published in 1774, which

[1] *Lloyd's E. P.*, March 9, 1774.

[2] *S. J. C.*, March 15, 1774; see *K. G.*, March 19, 1774.

[3] *M. J. & E. A.*, April 14, 1774; *Gaz.*, April 13, 1774.

[4] *S. J. C.*, Nov. 12, 1774.

[5] *L. C.*, Nov. 25, 1775.

was made up of a series of newspaper letters first published
in the *Public Advertiser,* over the signature "Constitutio."
In 1775 he wrote that he again presumed " to recommend
a parliamentary *Declaration of the Independency of the
American Colonies,* and then that there be formed by Means
of a general League, such an *Alliance* between us," as alone
in his opinion, could be " effectually and durably beneficial
to both Countries." He further stated, " It is true that I
stand almost alone on this Ground," and he acknowledged
that many men of the highest abilities stood against him
but no one of them, he alleged, had " that I know of, refuted my Arguments for the proposed Independency, or
those of Dean Tucker, which I have referred to." [1]   Cartwright, comparatively unknown at that time, received but a
fraction of the attention bestowed upon the older man.

The syllogistic reasoning of the anti-American group that
all subjects of Great Britain must pay taxes was sometimes
used by them in a different application.   Do you wish
America to be free; do you wish to see the colonies independent, they asked of those who denied that Parliament
had the right to tax the Americans?   One answer that was
frequently advanced was that Ireland, though not subject to
internal taxation by Parliament, was not independent.[2]   But
those who opposed American taxation did not rely chiefly
upon precedents.   Expediency, commercial expediency, was
their main reliance.   In the first place, however, it was noted
that the colonies were not allowed to pass laws repugnant to
the laws of England, and that the fact that the determination
of such repugnancy was left to the royal prerogative gave
the home country an efficient means of governing the colonies.[3]   Second, many maintained that America could be

---

[1] *P. A.,* Jan. 19, 1775.

[2] *S. J. C.,* Aug. 25, 1770; *M. J. & E. A.,* Oct. 13, 1774.

[3] *L. C.,* Nov. 28, 1765.

sufficiently governed and taxed by means of trade regulation. The famous Abbé Raynal was quoted in support of both of these views to the effect that " Great Britain enjoys all the power over her colonies that she ought to desire." [1] The holders of this second view were of opinion that colonies were valuable only for trade, and that therefore if their trade was not controlled " not one of the Ends " would be answered " for which those Colonies were planted." [2] Adherents of this plan were likely to assert that colonies were planted to provide markets, and were useful only as they did so. These were friends to the colonists insofar as the taxation issue was concerned, for they saw clearly that an America paying taxes would be able to pay less for goods, and that an America aggrieved because she was required to pay taxes that she thought unjust would make a poor customer. In addition, Americans thus taxed and thus aggrieved would begin to manufacture for themselves.

These were the people who delighted to quote Walpole to the effect that trade profits, not tax profits, should be extracted from America. One writer asserted that the whole trouble had arisen because England, in addition to controlling American trade, commerce and manufactures, now claimed the right to tax.[3] This combination of burdens, said another, was what made the colonial case extremely hard.[4] To quote another, " This is exactly the Dispute." [5]

The many who proposed that America should decide all matters of internal legislation while England should be content with regulating her trade, were in reality trying to gain

---

[1] *K. G.*, Oct. 11, 1775.

[2] *S. J. C.*, Jan. 13, 1770; *S. J. C.*, April 7, 1774.

[3] *M. J. & E. A.*, May 3, 1774.

[4] *L. P.*, Feb. 21, 1774.

[5] *P. A.*, May 3, 1774.

recognition for a quasi-federal system that had been long in operation within the empire. The essence of a federal system is in the division of powers among coordinate governments which are, in their places, controlled by a constitution; that is, in making a distinction between the different functions of government, such as the taxing power, or the power to regulate commerce; and in assigning the execution of these powers to different governmental bodies. The empire before 1763, when England made no pretense to tax America internally, but claimed and exercised the right to control her commerce, was federal in practice, though not in form; for certain powers had been administered by the home government and certain by the colonial, and because these powers were separate and distinct little clashing had taken place.[1] Most Englishmen, however, were unable to recognize the working organization of their empire. Blindly, they could not see that a federal system had been in operation, though some came so close they could hardly miss it. To many writers, a state had to be united under one legislature which exercised complete sovereignty in all cases; if any divisions of it were under the jurisdiction of local legislatures, exercising any powers to the exclusion of the central legislature, then they were not parts of the same state " but independent Nations " to which they had " no political affinity." [2] Sovereignty meant to them the location of all power in one body; they could not conceive of sovereignty distributed. "An Addresser at the London Tavern" contended that, "To admit the supremacy of this country . . . in all cases except . . . taxation, in which they say the Colonies are independent and uncontrolable, would be establishing *two sovereign*

---

[1] McLaughlin, *America and Britain* (New York, 1918) ; the chapter on The Background of American Federalism, gives a good discussion of the organization of the British Empire in the pre-revolutionary years.

[2] *S. J. C.,* Jan. 7, 1775.

authorities in one state, which is a contradiction." [1] A common argument was that "owning no Superior in one Instance, leads to the Disclaim of it in every other." If the colonies were granted their way in taxation, from that moment they would be a "distinct, separate Sovereignty," or at most they would be only in a " State of federal Subordination to Great Britain. A poor Hold indeed!" [2] " Messala " said that if the contentions of America were granted the empire would be " at best but a Confederacy of petty States." [3] These writers remind one of Thomas Hutchinson, who said, " I know of no line that can be drawn between the supreme authority of Parliament and the total independence of the colonies." [4]

England was declared to have preserved her liberty because she had one legislature only; if she had had more than one, as did France, and as the colonial advocates asked, then all her liberty would have disappeared, for with several assemblies there could be no working in concert. [5] " Messala " and his associates felt sure that unless the Americans were deprived of some of their liberties, the empire would become but a weak confederacy. A confederacy of states was perhaps a solution to the imperial problem, but he and his companions could not so see it. That they did not, however, was not because none in the English newspapers pointed it out.

During the Stamp Act agitation some very interesting letters signed "Æquus" contained a plea for the preservation of the system as it had existed. He wanted to know

[1] *L. C.,* Oct. 10, 1775.

[2] *S. J. C.,* March 17, 1774.

[3] *P. A.,* Feb. 20, 1775. This letter signed " Creon " was in *Lloyd's E. P.,* May 11, 1770.

[4] Bradford, *Mass. State Papers,* pp. 336, 340.

[5] *S. J. C.,* Aug. 12, 1775.

what motive there could be "to argue Americans out of their internal privileges," which could never properly interfere "with the external superiority of the mother state, nor at all affect her enjoyment of all the real advantages" that she could reasonably wish. He believed the colonies were entitled to all "legislative privileges, . . . for the conclusive regulating of their internal affairs"; but whether they were or not, "it would assuredly be the truest policy in the mother-state, . . . even formally to confirm the same to them. . . ." The reader will notice that this was not merely taxation but all legislation for internal affairs.[1] Even earlier, arguing from the clause, common in colonial charters, that "their laws should not be repugnant to those of Great Britain," he said it implied "as strongly as words and necessary incidents" could imply, "an exclusive legislative right in all internal cases that are consistent with them, and where no exceptions are reserved to the contrary. . . ."[2] "It is hard to conceive," he said, "from what constitutional principles applicable to a colony, not a conquered country, his [a colonist's] obedience to our statute law can be deduced."[3] "Brecknock" argued that, "Great Britain, each of the chartered colonies, and Ireland, are so many distinct STATES, each state having its own Great Council, over each of which Great Councils one and the same *Sovereign Power* presides; that *Sovereign Power* is the King of Great Britain, and the King of Great Britain only."[4]

In 1769 "A Briton" clearly had the idea and expressed it in a letter occasioned by the reading of a recent pamphlet, *The Case of Great Britain and America.* To him it appeared that the:

[1] *London Mag.,* Jan., 1766, p. 34; also in *L. C.,* Jan. 11, 1766.
[2] *L. C.,* Dec. 12, 1765.
[3] *L. C.,* Nov. 30, 1765.
[4] *Gaz.,* Oct. 28, 1768.

legislative power of the Colonies is divided. . . . Thus the Right of Legislation with Respect to Trade, which is the Means of acquiring Riches, resides solely in the Mother Country, . . . And on the other Hand, the Colonies have a right to every Branch of Legislation that does not belong to Trade or to Sovereignty, subject, however, to the Royal Assent or Dissent of whoever shall be King of England. . . . [1]

In 1775 a *Gentleman's Magazine* writer thought numberless advantages would accrue if some such accommodation could be made. " By it," he wrote, " a line might be drawn between internal and external taxation; between the powers of legislation in England and in America, in which the one could at no time clash with the other." [2]   Before this "Ludlow " had argued such a division of powers, for, said he, "A part may be supreme as to some articles of legislation; and another part of the constitution as to others." Some, he knew, would object that clashing would occur and that the different bodies would contradict each other. " But why so? If each is supreme in different ways, they cannot clash or contradict." [3]   Even if they sometimes should clash, he thought no greater mischief would result than from the successors of one legislature annulling the acts of its predecessor.   Plainly some writers understood the principles of federalism.

" Philanthropus " belonged to a small group that wanted to make the government of the colonies like that of Ireland.[4]   Others, seeing that something was wrong with the

---

[1] *S. J. C.,* Feb. 11, 1769. The pamphlet was by Gervase Parker Bushe, (Phila., 1769).

[2] *Gent. Mag.,* Nov., 1775, p. 545.

[3] *L. P.,* July 13, 1774; see *Gaz.,* Dec. 25, 1767. A pamphlet, *An Answer to a Pamphlet entitled Taxation No Tyranny,* "Addressed to the Author and Persons in Power. Just Published, Price 1s. 6d. Almon.," had a very clear discussion of federal principles. Large extracts were given in the *M. J. & E. A.,* April 1, 1775.

[4] *Gaz.,* Oct. 13, 1768; see *Gaz.,* June 17, Dec. 19, 1769.

existing imperial system but not taking kindly to the idea of making the colonial government similar to that of Ireland and being unable to conceive of an empire without one supreme parliament, thought to adjust the ill-working system by giving the Americans a representation in the British Parliament. Frequently the plan was to make no other change than the addition of American members, but sometimes the plans were more radical. Such notables as Grenville, Adam Smith, Franklin and Otis [1] considered the possibility of American representation in the British Parliament, and many lesser lights thought it might be the solution. As early as November, 1764, before the real troubles had begun, a *London Chronicle* paragraph stated that such a step " was certainly on the carpet." [2] A *St. James's Chronicle* writer, the next month, explained that the plan was to let the Americans have votes only in matters concerning America, but added that the plan was thought to be impracticable as it would set a precedent that the other parts of the empire would want to follow.[3] Though writers generally considered this plan unworkable and it was freely recognized that the Americans were by no means united in wanting it, it was continually advanced or spoken of as a possibility throughout the entire period.[4] Thomas Crowley, using the signature "Amor Patriae," was its chief newspaper advocate.[5]

---

[1] See R. G. Adams, *Political Ideas of the American Revolution,* p. 28, *et seq.;* Howard, *Preliminaries of the Am. Rev.,* p. 135.

[2] *L. C.,* Nov. 24, 1764.

[3] *S. J. C.,* Dec. 8, 1764.

[4] See *L. C.,* April 6, 1765, Jan. 14, Feb. 20, 1766, Aug. 27, Sept. 15, 1768, April 9, 1774, Jan. 28, Oct. 5, 12, 14, 1775; *S. J. C.,* April 9, Nov. 7, 1765, Feb. 18, 1766, March 15, 1774; *Lloyd's E. P.,* Dec. 26, 1774; *L. P.,* Dec. 28, 1774; *K. G.,* Jan. 14, 1772; *P. L.,* Aug. 30, 1765.

[5] See *S. J. C.,* Feb. 10, 22, 1774; see *Letters and Dissertations on Various Subjects,* by Thomas Crowley, where a number of his letters originally contributed to the papers are given. A penciled note on the Br. Museum

In 1774 the fourth article of the Declaration of the First Continental Congress contained the first official declaration of the final constitutional views of the Americans, that they were " entitled to a free and exclusive power of legislation, in their several provincial legislatures, . . . in all cases of taxation and internal policy, subject only to the negative of their sovereign," but that they would consent to *bona fide* acts for regulation of commerce. We have already seen this view in the argument by " Brecknock." When the Americans finally dropped this position they openly and avowedly picked up the standard of rebellion.

Late in 1765 "Æquus" took note that a similar argument had been advanced in England, when he wrote, " It has been asserted, that the King's Sceptre is the instrument of power over the Colonies, and Prerogative the rule by which their obedience must be regulated." [1] That he meant to include all legislation in this statement, with which he substantially agreed, seems probable, though a reading of some of his subsequent arguments leads one to think he may have meant to apply it to taxation only.[2] On February 4 of the next year a *St. James's Chronicle* paragraph reported that a great lawyer was of opinion that " taxing the Colonies was the sole prerogative of the Crown, and that the Legislature of this Kingdom " had " no Right to lay any Taxes thereon." [3] The assertion did not pass without notice and at least two letters in opposition to it were published.[4]

copy says it was published March 2, 1776. Francis Maseres wrote a pamphlet, published in 1770, *Considerations on the Expediency of Admitting Representatives from the American Colonies into the British House of Commons.*

[1] *Lloyd's E. P.,* Nov. 28 and Dec. 4, 1765.

[2] See letters signed " Æquus," probably by the same man in *London Mag.,* Jan., 1766 and in *L. C.,* Jan. 11, 1766.

[3] *S. J. C.,* Feb. 4, 1766.

[4] *S. J. C.,* Feb. 18, 1766; *L. C.,* Feb. 18, 1766.

It is somewhat less clear whether there were as early as this, supporters of colonial exemption from parliamentary legislation aside from taxation. That "Æquus" argued thus has been noted.[1] In 1768 "A Briton" wrote, "What very strongly marks the independence of the Americans on the British parliament is, that it has never been thought of, to make the House of Lords the ultimate resort in their appeals in law, as is the case from Ireland, the King in council remaining to this day sole arbiter."[2] By 1774 the argument was well known in England. A paragrapher complained that "the patriots of the nation," as the enemies of the administration and friends of the Americans were usually called, advocated such a solution, and asserted it would so augment the power of the crown that all liberty would be in danger.[3] "Who could believe," asked another paragrapher, "that patriotism could ever speak a language like this?" The crown was already far too strong, thought this observer, and the "patriots" were always declaiming against it, "Yet they now want to extend the influence of the Crown to a most enormous degree themselves, by supporting the claims of the Americans to throw off the Parliamentary authority of this country."[4] "Coriolanus" noted article four of the declaration of the congress and denounced it as subversive of all government.[5] It was plain that many Englishmen who were friendly to the colonists were not able to follow them on this point.

Perhaps the best statement of the American side of this

---

[1] *Supra*, pp. 119-120.

[2] *L. C.*, Oct. 20, 1768; see *Gaz.*, Sept. 24, Nov. 9, 1768.

[3] *L. P.*, March 11, 1774.

[4] *L. P.* and *M. J. & E. A.*, March 10, 1774; also in *M. C.*, March 10, 1774.

[5] *P. A.*, Jan. 5, 1775; see *Lloyd's E. P.*, Dec. 12, 1774; *L. C.*, April 11, 1767, Sept. 24, 1768.

argument was made by "Curtius."[1] He first made the prescriptive-right argument, stating that the alleged power of Parliament to levy internal taxation had been long unexercised; he based his main plea, however, on the fact that writs of error from the colonies had not gone to Parliament as they had in England and Scotland but had always gone to his majesty in council. Hence, the possessions of the Americans had not been considered as belonging to " *Subjects of this Kingdom,* all of whom are entitled to Trial by the ordinary Course of the Law "; but had " been considered as *Subjects of his Majesty."* He especially stressed the fact that colonial cases had not been tried " in the ordinary Course of the Law," as would have been the case if Parliament had had the legal supremacy.

The Gentlemen who contend for the supreme Legislature of Parliament over Persons residing in the Colonies are called upon to shew, how any Lawyer, from the 16th of King Charles to this Time, could have sat in Privy Council and examined and drawn into Question, determined, and disposed of the Lands, Tenements, Hereditaments, Goods and Chattels of the inhabitants of the several Colonies, if they had not (even to this Moment) denied them to *be Subjects of this Kingdom,* and consequently not subject to the internal Legislation, or taxation of Parliament.[2]

---

[1] Probably Dr. William Jackson, a London journalist; born in Ireland, who was sentenced to death for participation in the Irish rebellion of 1797 but committed suicide in prison; see article on Wm. Jackson in *Dic. Nat. Bio.* and Thomas MacNevin, *The Lives and Trials of Archibald Hamilton Rowan, the Rev. William Jackson etc.* (Dublin, 1846).

[2] *S. J. C.,* April 18, 1775; also in *G. E. P.,* April 13, 1775. Major Cartwright quoted this letter with approval in *American Independence,* appendix, p. 10. Edition of 1775.

CHAPTER VI

THE BISHOPS

The controversy over the introduction of Church of England bishops into the colonies found frequent expression in the papers.[1] Though the question was never so fiercely debated as were those which grew out of colonial taxation, it was still a matter of great importance and contributed much to the ill feeling developed in the colonies during the troubled years before actual hostilities began.[2] From the English viewpoint the question of episcopacy was more easily understood than some other American troubles because, to the dissenters in England, it was a matter of immediate moment. It was to some extent a domestic as well as a colonial problem. The opponents and advocates of the episcopal form of church government occasionally wrote letters to the papers, in which no mention of the colonies was made. The Presbyterians and their friends, especially, were opponents of episcopacy in any form, and consequently a section of the English public was prepared to appreciate and support the American objections to the introduction of bishops among them. This fellow feeling for the colonists among English dissenters may have been one of the reasons why Franklin, in July, 1773, writing of senti-

[1] The subject has been excellently treated by Cross in *The Anglican Episcopate and the American Colonies* (Harvard Historical Studies, 1902).

[2] See Hart, *American History Told by Contemporaries* (New York, 1908), vol. ii, p. 418; Van Tyne, *Causes of the American Revolution* (Boston, 1922), chap. iii; Tyler, *Lit. Hist. of the Am. Rev.* (New York, 1897), vol. i, p. 327.

ment in England to his friend Thomas Cushing reported, "The Dissenters are all for us."[1]

The prelates of the Church of England had long planned to establish bishops in the colonies so the issue was not a new one when the other American troubles began to assume importance. The project, dear to the hearts of zealous churchmen, was of sufficient general interest to get frequent mention in the public prints. Thus the *London Chronicle* reported the death of Paul Fisher, Esq., of Clifton near Bristol, who left among other bequests, one of " 1000£. for the use of the first bishop that shall be appointed in America;"[2] and a little later mentioned that the late Bishop of London had left £500 for the same purpose.[3]

The papers, besides taking notice of the desire for the establishment of bishops in the colonies, from time to time printed reports of jealousy and strife between the established church and dissenters in America. Thus the church was blamed for thwarting the missionary zeal of New England preachers, who had secured a charter for missionary work among the Indians only to have it made void, so said the allegation, by the influence of "some great ones of the Church of England." The writer of the letter, who asserted that he was no dissenter but a true Church of England man, objected to such selfish action, which, he said, showed the true character of the Church of England, whose business, it appeared was " not to propagate Christianity, but the Church of England; not to preach the Gospel to the poor Indians, but Episcopacy to the Presbyterians of New England." The grand point among them, he charged, was that of " epis-

[1] *Writings,* Smyth ed., vol. vi, p. 78.
[2] *L. C.,* March 1, 1763; see *London Mag.,* March-July, 1766.
[3] *L. C.,* July 5, 1764; see *ibid.,* June 23, Aug. 14, 1764.

copizing the Protestant churches in our colonies." This
critic of the church had been reading the views of Dr.
Mayhew, a famous American pamphleteer in the episcopacy controversy, and agreed with him.[1]   J. Philiber also
took note of the alleged obstruction of New England
missionary enterprise and thought it a great evil.[2]   In a
succeeding letter he vigorously denounced the plans for
bishops in America.[3] The allegation of "dog in the
manger" tactics by the Church of England was frequently made.   Some critic or critics of the Anglican
Church saw fit to print a few words of admonition to the
episcopal leaders, in the following words:

The Leaders in the episcopal Society for propagating the Gospel
in foreign parts may consider, whether it might not be more
proper to employ their wisdom and revenue, for some years,
in recovering their own thinn'd flocks from Popery, than in
Missions abroad, and in episcopizing Protestant Dissenters, and
converting the Indians.[4]

This was printed in a prominent corner of the *London
Chronicle* and appeared at irregular intervals during the
years 1764 and 1765.

The position of the Church of England in the matter
is easily understood.   It was the proud state church of a
proud England, of an England which habitually spoke of
the American colonies as "our" colonies, "our" possessions.   In America were many communicants and
many churches needing supervision.   Until the church
in America had a hierarchy of bishops its organization
would be incomplete and its effectiveness impaired.   Be-

---

[1] *L. C.*, Jan. 17, 1764; see *ibid.*, Jan. 21, Feb. 11, 1764.

[2] *S. J. C.*, Feb. 25, 1764; see *Gaz.*, May 16, 1769.

[3] *S. J. C.*, May 26, 1764; see *Mass. Hist. Soc. Collections*, vol 78, p.
104; *S. J. C.*, Aug. 11, 1768.

[4] *L. C.*, Feb. 16, 1764, *passim*.

sides, the missionary zeal of the church was easily stirred
by the opportunity to convert the Indians. The Church
of England, like most virile institutions, wished to propagate its faith, to seek new converts, to grow. " Crito "
expressed a common argument, when he accused the
American opponents of bishops with unreasonableness
and intolerance.

But, alas! of what manner of spirit can those men be, who
would deny the established church those privileges, that toleration, which they themselves enjoy both in Europe and America;
the privilege, I mean, of ordaining Pastors among themselves
without the hazard, expence and delay of being obliged to cross
the Atlantic for holy orders! That this is the principal object
for which an American bishop is wished and desired, the Americans have been so repeatedly assured, by the best authorities,
that skepticism itself can scarcely doubt it. And till such an
establishment is effected, America exhibits a phaenomenon unknown in the Christian world; the religion by law established
in the Mother Country exists, or rather languishes there in
an imperfect, a mutilated state. . . . [1]

The letter above quoted from was printed in 1768, but
practically the same arguments were used in a letter with
the same signature in 1764.[2] " Il Modrato " stressed
similar arguments. This need of a bishop, resident in
America, to do away with the necessity of the long voy-
age to England, was especially emphasized.

What would the Presbyterians there say, if their People were
obliged to come over hither for Ordination? which is the Case
of the poor Episcopalians, Numbers of whom have lost their
Lives in the Expedition. And why is the Church of England
to be the only Church upon Earth that ever suffered her flocks

---

[1] *L. C.*, Aug. 27, 1768; see *Gent. Mag.*, June, 1769, p. 292.
[2] *Lloyd's E. P.*, March 14, 1764; see *ibid.*, Aug. 27, 1764.

to want Shepherds, when there was a possibility of sending them? [1]

To "Moderato," another advocate of bishops, it seemed a simple question of toleration on the part of the Americans. If the Church of England desired a bishop in America "instead of a Lay Commissary from the Bishop of London, what Friend to Toleration can refuse his Assent to so very reasonable a Request?"[2] Such writers, in seeking to throw a charge of intolerance upon the Americans, made out a case that seemed eminently reasonable. If this had been all, the colonists would have been in a position difficult to maintain. It was, however, a presentation that left much to be desired on the score of completeness, one that took no account of several important factors, notably of the method by which the proposed bishops were to be supported and of certain strong antipathies inherited by most of the colonial dissenters.

These factors, which the more diplomatic among the advocates of American bishops avoided as far as possible, were emphasized by opponents of the scheme, who were better represented in the papers than were the advocates. We have seen with what spirit " Crito " assured his readers that bishops were wanted chiefly for the purpose of facilitating the ordination of colonial clergymen without the necessity of having them come to England for the laying on of hands. Repeated assurances by the authorities supported his declaration, but still some skeptics would not or could not believe that this was the whole of the story. At least one Englishman, "A Country

[1] *S. J. C.*, Nov. 28, 1765; an answer Dec. 7, 1765; and a supporting letter Dec. 12, 1765; see *ibid.*, May 28 and June 2, 1767.

[2] *S. J. C.*, Jan. 14, 1766; see *Gaz.*, June 27 and July 8, 1769.

Clergyman," took the position that bishops were not necessary in America for the ordination of clergymen there. He argued that bishops were invested with their powers by the state; that the powers they exercised were from the state; and that therefore the Bishop of London could send commissaries to America with as much right to confer orders as the bishop himself.[1] Such an argument, being contrary to the church's teaching, was not tenable, as "Favenius" pointed out a short time later.[2]

Most opponents of bishops in America, however, were so silent respecting this argument that it was a great inconvenience for the Anglicans in America to have no resident bishops that we may consider the point granted. The objections to American bishops on the part of Englishmen were for the most part either opportunist, or founded on a belief that the church was, as an institution, a tool of authority, an institution capable of being used as a strong weapon for an oppressive government. Not only did many fear that there was danger in the colonies, but some insisted there was a menace at home.

The fact that the Americans strongly objected to the presence of bishops amongst them no Englishman could reasonably doubt; and accordingly it was rarely challenged. "A. B.," however, felt sure that the accounts of American antagonism to bishops were exaggerated, as he thought a great many gentlemen in the colonies, especially in Virginia and Maryland "would look upon it as a great blessing to have a learned, discreet, and pious Bishop residing among them, as it is what they have long earnestly wished for."[3] The writer of an

[1] *L. C.*, Sept. 21, 1768.
[2] *S. J. C.*, Oct. 6, 1768.
[3] *P. L.*, Oct. 28, 1765.

American letter in the *Public Advertiser*, however, said
that he firmly believed "the Sight of Lawn Sleeves here
would be more terrible to us than ten thousand Mohawks,
or the most savage Indians in this Quarter of the Globe."[1]
George Burn, a young Englishman traveling in America,
wrote to his father in London that the Americans would
never endure episcopacy and that the British ministry
well knew that as long as the Americans kept free from
bishops they would love civil liberty.[2]   Other messages
from America to the same effect were frequent.

"Philocolonus" pointed out the objections to episcopacy which the Americans, together with many Englishmen who had stayed in England, had inherited from the
previous century.   He referred to attempts to establish
American bishops in the time of Laud and at a later
date, charging, "In both Cases, the State and Church
seem to have cooperated in the hopeful Work of hum-
bling the Colonists."   The same motive, he thought,
was again at work, and but for a recent overthrow of the
ministry the Americans might have had bishops.   The
advocates of bishops, he said, were very modest, but this
had not deceived the colonists, who very well knew "that
where Episcopal Power once gets in a Finger,. it will
soon make way for the Hand and the Arm, and, by degrees for the whole Body."[3]

The first period of prominence for the episcopacy
question in the pre-revolutionary era coincided with the
Stamp Act controversy.   During the first few months
of 1765 paragraphs appeared in various papers stating
that the introduction of bishops into America was soon

[1] *P. A.*, Jan. 29, 1768.

[2] *L. P.*, Jan. 4, 1775 and *M. C.*, Jan. 4, 1775.

[3] *S. J. C.*, Aug. 8, 1765.

to be investigated,[1] or that much opposition would meet "the motion for introducing Church Dignitaries in North America."[2] If the scheme was adopted, the Rev. Mr. George Whitefield was to be appointed to one of the bishoprics,[3] while an earlier notice said Dean Tucker was likely to be appointed Bishop of Albany.[4] Another paragraph, treating the establishment of bishops in America as settled, informed the public that a delegation of eminent clergymen first would be sent to America to "make an enquiry into the general state of Religion at that place."[5] To some, these signs of life in the episcopacy question, coming at that particular time, were not a coincidence.

A few writers made a connection with the "most arbitrary and obnoxious" measures being pursued in America. "A Christian" wrote, "We have been told, . . . of their complaints against the Stamp Act, and Admirality Courts; . . . but there is . . a still greater lurking Evil . . . the Establishment of a lordly Prelacy." He related how it was the fear of a prelacy in the days of Laud that drove many of the colonists to America.[6] "Americanus," a little later asserted that it "may be undeniably proved, that a great Share of the present Alarms and Commotions in our Northern American Colonies, is owing to the Scheme of establishing an ecclesiastical Hierarchy amongst them; . . ." It was the dread of this scheme, "aided by some other unhappy Causes"

[1] *L. C.,* April 2, 1765; see *S. J. C.,* Jan. 29, 1765.

[2] *Lloyd's E. P.,* Feb. 11, 1765.

[3] *S. J. C.,* March 19, 1765.

[4] *S. J. C.,* March 20, 1764.

[5] *Lloyd's E. P.,* April 1, 1765; *L. C.,* April 2, 1765.

[6] *S. J. C.,* Oct. 31, 1765.

that had driven the people to despair.[1] "No Powow" made a similar charge when the Stamp Act trouble was at its highest, reminding his readers that, "it should never be forgotten that these distresses" had been first "brought on, and uncommonly aggravated, by the Apprehensions of a prelatical Hierarchy at their Door, and ready to be run in upon them."[2]

These assertions were so frequent in the London papers during the Stamp Act period that Dr. Thomas Bradbury Chandler, a colonist, and a warm advocate of episcopacy in America, took occasion in a pamphlet, *The Appeal to the Public in Behalf of the Church of England in America*, which he published in 1767, to reject as without foundation the statements made in some English newspapers at the time of the Stamp Act "to the effect that the discontent and uneasiness manifested by the colonists on that occasion were due in a great measure to the fear that bishops would be settled among them." He argued that the colonists were discontented only because of an "alleged unconstitutional act."[3]

Shortly after the repeal of the Stamp Act, "Homologistes" wrote that when the late Tory ministry had decided upon the humiliation of America, they had thought it would not be decent to exclude the churchmen from a share of despotism over the Americans and, "Accordingly the Stamping and Episcopizing our Colonies were understood to be only different Branches of the same Plan of Powers."[4] Others made the same connection between episcopacy and toryism. "An Unchangeable

---

[1] *S. J. C.*, Nov. 23, 1765; see Jan. 2, 1766.

[2] *S. J. C.*, Feb. 11, 1766.

[3] See Cross, *Anglican Episcopate*, p. 170; *P. L.*, Oct. 28, 1765.

[4] *S. J. C.*, June 14, 1766.

Whig," writing a letter taking the American side of the case, asserted that, "To trace the Progress of Toryism in Church and State from the Year 1746 to the present Times, would require a Volume of no small size."[1] Another correspondent insisted that the colonists had good reason to fear the introduction of bishops among them for they would come allied with the state and it was this "union of church and state power, that drove the first settlers into those remote parts of the globe." They had suffered persecution once and might suffer it again.

With the dying down of all interest in America after the repeal of the Stamp Act much less was found in the papers regarding colonial bishops. The matter, however, was not settled; it was simply quiescent. In July, 1768, the papers reported that the episcopacy controversy was raging furiously in America, and with this recrudescence of interest there came a response in England.[3] For the remainder of the period frequent, though irregular notice, was taken of the controversy, but the interest shown was never any greater than it was during the Stamp Act period.

"Atlanticus" well stated the American objections to bishops. He thought, with Franklin,[4] that the civil government was little likely to force bishops upon the reluctant colonists; but he was certain that the ambitious ecclesiastics would keep the project alive. The American objections, he thought, might be summed up under two heads. First, they were not unmindful or

---

[1] *S. J. C.,* Jan. 21, 1766.

[2] *Lon. Mag.,* July, 1766, p. 354.

[3] *S. J. C.,* July 23, 1768; *L. C.,* June 21, 1768; see *Gaz.,* July 23, 1768, May 26, 25, 5, 1769.

[4] *Writings,* Smyth ed., vol. v, pp. 133-134.

forgetful of that "galling yoke, which forced their fore-fathers from their native country into the unhospitable deserts of America."[1]   This objection was especially strong in the Puritan colonies. Second, the objection was to bishops supported by state taxes. He supposed that every Englishmen would own that the Americans had reason to be "alarmed at the State-Episcopacy, which Dr. B. Chandler threatens them with."[2] The Americans could have no objections to the few Episco-palians in their midst having bishops of their own, pro-vided they were not supported by a tax which would fall upon some Christians who held bishops to be unlawful and unscriptural. The prospect that the bishops would be supported by taxes brought the question into the main stream of American difficulties and made appli-cable to it all the objections to taxation without repre-sentation.

To some Englishmen, bishops in America seemed necessary as an aid to government control. These openly advocated bishops because, once established, they would make easier the governing of the unruly colo-nists.[3] Such pleas for bishops were sure to rouse the most strenuous colonial objections. One paragrapher thought the lack of American bishops and the want of an established church in America the main cause of all the disturbances there. He quoted Bishop Warburton with approval to the effect that no state could exist without an alliance with the church. The Boston Port Bill being under discussion at the time, the writer strongly urged that with it be coupled a bill to intro-duce bishops, as no time could be so propitious as the

[1] *L. C.,* June 28, 1768; see *ibid.,* June 1, 1771.
[2] *L. C.,* July 26, 1768; see *Gaz.,* July 30, Sept. 30, 1768.
[3] *Gaz.,* April 6, 1774.

present.[1] A little later another writer, in the same vein, urged the immediate appointment of bishops for America with all the ordinances of the Church of England, "not so much from any religious predilection in its favour, as on the supposition, or rather demonstration, that its principles and tenets have, by the experience of two centuries and upwards, been found to correspond best with the genius of a limited monarchy: whence the proverb, *No Bishop, No King!*"[2] This writer was well aware that the Americans would object, but he would have no attention paid to their wishes.

"Irenaeus Episcophilus" went even further. With a curiously blind misreading of Bostonian character, he urged that "a true Christian Bishop be established at Boston, with Presbyters and Deacons." Such advice, he assured his readers, was good and would improve conditions. "Spiritual unity is altogether as necessary as political unity. The Church, the senior, and the State, the junior sister, will live in delectative harmony."[3] It is a little hard to believe that any Englishman was blind enough to give credence to such sentiments, but blindness almost as great was common among English leaders. Perhaps "Irenaeus Episcophilus" was an enemy to the episcopizing plan and wrote such a bald statement of the case in order to stir up resistance. He could scarcely have uttered words better calculated to rouse colonial antagonism.

The English, then, who objected to the episcopizing of the colonies were the more ready to urge that side of the question because of a widespread belief among dissenters

[1] *P. A.*, March 29, 1774; also in *Lloyd's E. P.*, March 30, 1774.

[2] *Lloyd's E. P.*, May 9, 1774; see *ibid.*, May 6, 11, 1774; *Gaz.*, March 30, 1774.

[3] *L. C.*, April 14, 1774.

that episcopacy and tyranny were related. This feeling was sometimes shared even by the more liberal among the Church of England itself. Others among the dissenters looked upon episcopacy as an unlawful institution, one unwarranted by scripture and even contrary to scripture. These would have abolished the institution in England if they could have gained an opportunity, but seeing no hope of achieving that result, they were eager to prevent the spread of a system they so much hated and feared. Others, perhaps, although neutral on the question of episcopacy, well knew American objections to it and would have readily approved a writer in the *London Chronicle* who wrote, "There are dissentions enough already in America. Our governors want not to increase, but to pacify them."[1] This last feeling probably had the most weight in causing the government to proceed slowly with the matter.[2]

[1] *L. C.*, Feb. 6, 1769; see *ibid.*, July 2, 1768, Sept. 8. 1770; *Gaz.*, Sept. 8, 1768.

[2] The controversy did not stop in 1775 for Francis Maseres, over the signature "F. M." saw fit to write a letter to the *P. A.*, March 24, 1778, on the *Inexpediency of Establishing Bishops in North America;* see Francis Maseres, *Occasional Essays on Various Subjects* (London, 1809). There is another essay on the bishop question in the same collection but it does not appear that it was printed in a newspaper.

CHAPTER VII

THE TOWNSHEND ACTS

On February 17, 1767, the British Parliament voted to reduce the land tax by one shilling in the pound. This necessitated the raising of new revenues for the royal treasury. That task fell to the lot of Charles Townshend, chancellor of the exchequer. In the middle of March a newspaper correspondent noted that the land tax was the "chief topick of conversation."[1] A paragraph said America was to be taxed "to make good the £500,000 taken off the Land-tax."[2] Near the end of the month an anonymous writer felt moved to publish a statement showing that the Americans paid their share of taxes already because it appeared attempts were being made "to connect our colonies in America with the reduction of the land tax, in such a manner" as he was afraid might "tend to disagreement and confusion," but could "neither benefit them, nor the *mother country*."[3] In May the connection was made, for the Townshend Acts were passed. Thus the American controversy was reopened.

The period of the greatest agitation over the Stamp Act had lasted from about the middle of October, 1765, until April, 1766; by June of that year nothing but echoes of the strife was to be heard. During the main part of the period indicated, the American troubles,

[1] *L. C.,* March 14, 1767.
[2] *Gaz.,* March 7, 1767.
[3] *L. C.,* March 28, 1767; see *S. J. C.,* April 9, 1767.

growing out of the Stamp Act supplied the chief topic
of discussion in the press.   The question was important;
the printers realized its importance and gave it commensurate space.   The Townshend Acts, however, never became so absorbing a topic to the papers.   In total probably more was printed about them than about the Stamp
Act, but they were never at any one time so exclusively
the topic of the day as the Stamp Act had been.

Two factors especially may help to explain this.   In
the first place, the earliest American resistance to the
Townshend Acts, taking the form of non-importation
agreements drawn up in meeting, lacked the dramatic
character of the Stamp Act riots.   By this time too, the
English were somewhat habituated to hearing bad news
from the colonies.   Second, the Stamp Act troubles had
come during a period of quiet in English political life.
No other issues got enough newspaper mention to de-
tract from the interest paid to them.   This situation was
certainly reversed in the case of the Townshend Acts, for
the period during which they were on the English law
books was one of the most distracted in English political life.   Chief among the distractions must be mentioned those connected with the name of that popular
idol, rascal and advancer of liberty, John Wilkes.   From
the spring of 1768, when he returned to London from
Paris, whence he had fled some four years previously, he
was for a few years the most prominent citizen of the
land, if newspaper mention is the criterion.   This was
also the period which saw the publication of the most
remarkable and famous anonymous newspaper letters of
English history, the letters of "Junius," which doubled
the circulation of the *Public Advertiser*, the paper in
which they were first printed, and must be ranked as one
of the great political forces of the time.   The affairs of

the East India Company also received a very great deal of attention during these years.

Like the Stamp Act, the Townshend Acts gained little space in the papers until the news of the unfavorable reception in America began to reach England. In the spring of 1767 something of a campaign was made in favor of them by the printing of representations that the Americans were remiss in the matter of tax paying.[1] In April "A friend to Both Countries" claimed that every step was being taken to enrage Englishmen against the Americans. "Pamphlets and newspapers," he wrote, "flie about, and coffee-houses ring with lying reports."[2] "Benevolus"[3] and "F. B."[4] made similar charges. Franklin, in a letter to Joseph Galloway, written in August, is authority for the statement that every effort was being made at that time to render American taxation popular, by insisting on American wealth and the great load of British taxes,[5] such a campaign having added cogency just then because of the prevailing hard times in England. Letters from America were said to be full of apprehensions "lest new taxation" should "produce new disorders."[6] Not much material, however, got into the papers; and on the whole American affairs were dismissed very lightly during 1767. The hard times in England received much more space, and there even seemed to be a disposition to regard American affairs as settled.

A large number of letters and paragraphs told of the

[1] See *Gaz.*, Feb. 20, March 5, 9, April 13, 18, June 1, 1767.

[2] *L. C.*, April 9, 1767; see *Gaz.*, Feb. 6, 1767.

[3] *L. C.*, April 11, 1767.

[4] *L. C.*, April 9, 1767; see *Gaz.*, Feb. 10, 1767.

[5] *Writings*, Smyth, vol. v, pp. 41-42; see *ibid.*, pp. 75, 91.

[6] *Gent. Mag.*, May, 1767, p. 278.

currency shortage in America.   Perhaps this was in part an effort to combat the idea that the Americans were very rich.[1]

On October 28, 1767, a Boston town meeting, called on account of the Townshend Acts, passed non-importation resolutions, thus opening a movement that was soon to become general.   On December 11 the first accounts of the Boston agreement were printed in the English papers, and as non-importation was a subject of never-failing interest to the English printers, the news speedily caused more comment than any other American news for the year.   Perhaps as a coincidence the same number of the *Whitehall Evening Post* that carried the news of the Boston action also reported that business was so bad in Birmingham that upwards of three hundred workmen had been discharged.[2]   Paragraphs told of the stimulus these agreements would give to American manufacturers or simply announced the establishment of manufactures in the colonies, giving the inference that these were in-direct results of the acts.   According to one account, encouragement from Boston and Philadelphia was being given to induce Glasgow and Paisly workmen to migrate, while factories for cloth, firearms and various other articles were reported to be growing up in America.[3]   Americans were said to be brewing beverages from native shrubs to prevent the use of "unwholesome ex-oticks."[4]

"Old England" and "No Bostonian" showed well the old mercantile attitude in regard to colonies when they

[1] See *Gaz.*, Feb. 10, 16, June 13, 1767, Nov. 24, 1768.

[2] *W. E. P.*, Dec. 12, 1767.

[3] *P. A.*, Jan. 2, Feb. 1, 1768; see *Gaz.*, Dec. 14, 1767; *London Mag.*, Appendix, 1767, p. 681; *Univ. Mag.*, Dec., 1767, p. 334.

[4] *W. E. P.*, Dec. 31, 1767; see *Lloyd's E. P.*, May 26, 1769.

wrote bitter letters on the situation. "Old England," for example, thought that the Americans, in manufacturing, were going expressly contrary to the purpose of colonization. He felt that in time Americans would inevitably begin to manufacture, but it was unfortunate that they had begun so soon. He believed it would be possible to tax American manufactures so that the colonists could not bring them "to market cheaper than ours."[1] A *Lloyd's Evening Post* letter was significantly headed, "The Woolen and Iron Manufactures not in Danger from the Resolutions of the Colonists."[2]

Despite efforts to assure readers that the resolutions at Boston were not dangerous, that they were the work of a "dying faction"[3] and that the attention given to them was out of proportion to their real importance, the abuse they caused to be heaped upon the Bostonians, and the statements made in regard to the very great importance of American trade,[4] belied such attempts. The English traders were being injured in their pocketbooks, and they were apprehensive of still greater injuries.

In the early part of 1768 the papers were giving more and more space to the colonial situation, and it might have become the outstanding subject in them, had not the return of Wilkes to England and his election to the House of Commons in March furnished a domestic problem seemingly of much more importance. In the flood of letters over Wilkes and the general election, the American troubles dropped out of sight.

[1] *Lloyd's E. P.,* Dec. 18, 1767.

[2] *Lloyd's E. P.,* July 1, 1768.

[3] *Lloyd's E. P.,* Dec. 16, 1767; see *Gaz.,* Jan. 19, 1768.

[4] *Lloyd's E. P.,* Jan. 13, 1768 and *P. A.,* Jan. 8, 1768; see *Gaz.,* Jan. 28, 1768.

The Massachusetts Circular Letter of February 11, 1768, stirred up some comment in the press. "Pro Patria" spoke of it as a measure, "so daring, so artful," and one that had "such a tendency to inflame and incite the people to contemn the legal authority of Parliament . . ."[1] That it received so little was probably due to the immense excitement over John Wilkes, for during the months when the letter might reasonably have been prominent in the papers, in March, April, May and June, the Wilkes affair was at fever heat. On March 28 he was elected to Parliament by Middlesex; on May 10 took place the Massacre of St. George's Field; and on June 18 he was sentenced to serve twenty-two months in prison.[2] Some comment was made on the letter, however, and the controversy between Governor Bernard and the Massachusetts Assembly was well reported, although opinion on it was scanty.[3]

Wilkes was safely in prison and the interest in him was dying down when the Boston tax riots of June, 1768, in which the affair of the sloop, Liberty, loomed so prominently, again brought American news to the fore. This news, coming at a slack period in news sensations, was well played up in the press and during August, September, October and into November news from beyond the Atlantic had the leading place. In August the *Gentleman's Magazine*, giving the unusual number of five pages to the American situation, in its headings spoke of the "critical situation" there and of the "fall in stocks occasioned by the disagreeable news."[4] The

---

[1] *Lloyd's E. P.*, Sept. 21, 1768.

[2] As one writer said, "For many years past England has not been disturbed with so many commotions at one time." *Gaz.*, May 14, 1768.

[3] See *Gent. Mag.*, May, June, Aug., 1768; see *London Mag.*, June, 1768.

[4] *Gent. Mag.*, Aug., 1768, p. 357 *et seq.*

letter writers who since the spring of 1766 had relegated American affairs to an almost negligible place, once more began to consider them. The whole situation was soon the subject of lively discussion in the newspapers. In November and December the Middlesex election and the East India Company crowded it out; for the remainder of the Townshend Acts period American issues were prominent, even though the debate was never at fever heat.

From the first breath of American troubles in 1765 traces of bitterness had not been lacking in the letters of those who wrote against the colonists, but, as the dissensions became chronic, the bitterness increased. American troubles were no longer an incident; they were an ever-present issue. Sides were forming, and politics was being played more and more.

It was frequently rumored, early in August, that harsh measures were to be taken against the Americans; some thought war might possibly result, for the administration was aroused. "Caius Memmius" wrote that he had long refused to believe such reports, but that of late he was being forced reluctantly to do so, as they were "daily reiterated in the papers."[1] He very much deplored such a prospect. "Meanwell," remarking that the Boston disturbances were the chief topic of public conversation, argued that they had been caused by the Commissioners of Revenue, sent over by England, and that the Bostonians should not be too severely condemned.[2] "Moderator" deprecated the epithets and abuse being heaped upon all Americans, for he felt that the acts of a mob influenced by a madman or two should not be credited to the account of all the Americans.

[1] *S. J. C.*, Aug. 16, 1768; see *S. J. C.*, Aug. 23, 1768.
[2] *P. A.*, July 28, 1768.
[3] *P. A.*, Aug. 3, 1768.

"Tranquillus" declared, "It makes one's whole Frame tremble to think, that because the Americans cannot submit to what is absolutely unconstitutional, they must be bombarded, butchered, and see their fine Towns reduced to Ashes!" Chastisement, he thought, might make them slaves, but it could never convince their understandings.[1]

Early in 1766 there was a little controversy over the creation of the office of Secretary of State for the Colonies, an office first filled by Lord Hillsborough. Some argued that this action simply showed that the real reason for all the American troubles was the creation by the administration of a large number of placemen both at home and in America in the expectation that these officeholders would support the government in difficulties.[2] "Caius Memmius" and "Expositer"[3] both assured the public that this was the real reason for American taxation, and this charge was frequently repeated after 1768.[4]

That the Americans were not without strong support at this period may be gathered from an article in the *London Magazine*. This periodical gave almost a page to the dispute raging between Governor Bernard and the Massachusetts Bay Assembly, and at the end of the account made a statement in parenthesis from which the following is taken:

In short there is such just and cogent reasoning, such a spirit of liberty breathes through the whole of the American productions, at this time, as would not have disgraced antient Greece

[1] *S. J. C.*, Aug. 4, 1768.

[2] *Gaz.*, Jan. 12, 1768; see two answering letters *Gaz.*, Jan. 21, 1768.

[3] *London Mag.*, Aug., 1768, p. 429; *L. C.*, Sept. 29, 1768 respectively.

[4] See *L. C.*, Oct. 29, 1768; *Gent. Mag.*, Dec., 1775, p. 564; *L. P.*, Feb. 1, 1775; *S. J. C.*, April 7, 1774; *P. A.*, May 23, 1775.

or Rome, when struggling against oppression: at the same time that the authors and abbettors of the present impolitick measures in England, are as to argument and language, even below contempt. They are absolutely taking steps against the colonies that might have been expected from our princes and their wretched ministers in the 17th century, but rather disgrace the present reign, so distinguished for its blessings and its protecting the subject in the enjoyment of liberty and property. From our own observations we will venture to say, that nine persons in ten, even in this country, are friends to the Americans and thoroughly convinced they have right on their side.[1]

Whatever allowance may be made for partisan heat and for exaggeration, it is certain that when one of the leading monthly magazines of the kingdom spoke in such vein, there must have been some grounds for it. Supporting evidence was not lacking, as has been noted above. An unsigned letter said it was a "singular circumstance, that whoever is hardy enough to maintain the cause of Great Britain, against subjects, who disown her authority, or to raise his voice in defence of the laws and constitution, is immediately pointed out to the public for Mr. Grenville's friend."[2]

Others pointed out that the Americans were simply claiming one exemption after another. "Mentor," in a series of letters, exposed "the insidius Artifice of the New Englanders" in doing so, and then in basing their new claim on the ground conceded to them in the former. First, they claimed a distinction between external and internal taxes, and as soon as internal ones were given up, external ones became insupportable. Then they progressively urged that taxes could be levied only by the consent of the taxed, and that this consent

---

[1] *London Mag.*, Aug., 1768, pp. 439-440.
[2] *Gent. Mag.*, Aug., 1768, p. 357.

could be given only by representatives elected by them. From this they complained about laws made without their own consent, and finally they cried out against trade regulations.[1]

In this period much interest was also taken in the non-importation resolutions of the colonists. "Verax" belittled the danger of non-importation with arguments that had a wide recognition in England.[2] He maintained that Americans could not compete with English manufacturers for at least a century because American wages were so high, and that they were bound to remain high as long as there was plenty of good cheap land in the colonies. No man would work for low wages when there was land to be had almost for the asking. He asserted that artisans who migrated to America soon became farmers.[3] Franklin had made this view known in England.[4]

Another common view was expressed by "Pro Patria." He wanted all current manufacturing stopped and any new manufacturing prohibited in the colonies if they were to pay no taxes. This, he said, was only right for if they were "to be exempted from paying taxes, . . . on account of their purchasing manufactures from us, they ought to be restrained from engaging in them."[5] This, of course, was in answer to the argument that the colonists were sufficiently taxed by being forced to purchase manufactures from England.

The harmlessness of the non-importation measures was

---

[1] *P. A.*, Nov. 3, 1768; see *P. A.*, Nov. 25, 1774; *M. C.*, Dec. 10, 1774; *Gaz.*, Dec. 22, 1767.

[2] See Schlesinger, *Colonial Merchants*, p. 20n.

[3] *Lloyd's E. P.*, Aug. 12, 1768; see *Gaz.*, Dec. 22, 1767.

[4] *L. C.*, April 21, 1774.

[5] *Lloyd's E. P.*, Sept. 19, 1768.

dwelt upon so frequently by the anti-American writers, that one is moved to suggest that they protested too much. "A Briton" answered those who argued that the Americans could not keep such non-importation agreements because their need of British manufactures and the love of gain would drive them to import goods, and because men would find means to pursue "profit, in spite of every regulation to the contrary. . . ." He felt that those who argued thus failed to take into account the lasting power of resentment, and also neglected to consider that the colonists might succeed, despite the utmost efforts of the government, in smuggling in such manufactures as they needed from other sources.[1]

A change was coming into newspaper writing in that it seemed less spontaneous than formerly. Now a few great pseudonyms were established with the public, and long series of letters from the same pen were common. "Old Mentor" became one of the most prominent of the anti-American writers.[2] At first, being much irritated at the Americans, he suggested that all trade be cut off in retaliation, a measure sufficient, he thought, to show "these Braggarts their Insignificancy in the Scale of Empire, . . ."[3] Before long, however, when it appeared that if the colonists should succeed they would do so only with great effort, he assured the public, in a series of letters, that non-importation was of little moment. He said it was out of character for merchants to sacrifice their private good for public welfare, and that all the ages could not "produce an Instance of a Society of trading Patriots" who entered into such agreements

[1] *L. C.,* Oct. 20, 1768.

[2] The anti-American letters of "Old Mentor" and the pro-American letters of "The Colonist's Advocate" feature this period.

[3] *P. A.,* Oct. 1, 1768.

and "were faithful in the Performance." To show that
the Boston merchants were no exception to the rule he
quoted much from " John Maine," a printer of Boston,
meaning undoubtedly the redoubtable John Mein, who
pointed to some flagrant double dealing by the Boston
merchants.   And, he asserted, New York merchants had
done likewise.   Such charges were common.[1]   He maintained that the agreements had had no sensible effect
upon the manufacturers of England, either because they
were very laxly enforced or because the trade with
America was of much less consequence than it was popularly supposed to be.[2]

By the autumn of 1769 every colony except New
Hampshire, following the leadership of Massachusetts,
had adopted non-importation agreements.[3]   Not only
did these cause considerable newspaper discussion, but
the papers followed the successive steps with so much
fullness, that no well-informed Englishmen had excuse
for not knowing the situation.

An incident which occured during the period of the
Townshend Acts, though it did not grow directly out of
them, was the Boston Massacre of March 5, 1770.   A
number of writers had previously pointed out that the
presence of troops in Boston was likely to lead to out-
breaks.[4]   The first reports were printed in the *Public
Advertiser* of April 23, and the affair was soon ade-
quately and fairly reported in the papers.   The American
side, which was printed first, consisted of extracts,
printed at length, from the Boston *Gazette* of March 20.[5]

[1] See *Gaz.*, Oct. 24, 17, 1768.

[2] *P. A.*, Dec. 13, 1769; see also *P. A.*, Nov. 30, Dec. 22, 1769, Jan. 30,
1770 and other letters; see *Gaz.*, Jan. 16, June 21, 1770 *passim*.

[3] Schlesinger, *op. cit.*, p. 156.

[4] *P. A.*, Oct. 25, 27, 28, Nov. 1, 1769.

[5] *Lloyd's E. P.*, April 23, 1770; *P. A.*, April 23, 24, 1770.

This was followed shortly by accounts giving the soldiers' version. Though a number of letters and paragraphs were printed about the affair, it did not become more than a minor topic of the day. A false report, stating that a mob had killed Captain Preston and the soldiers concerned in the massacre, was printed,[1] and on August 25 the *Public Advertiser* printed a long and careful Boston statement, protesting vigorously against alleged misrepresentations of Boston in the English press, and referring especially to the *Public Advertiser* account of April 28, called the "Case of Captain Preston," which, on Preston's own testimony, had been so changed as seriously to misrepresent. A letter written by Preston, March 12, 1770, was printed to prove the point. While there had been much misrepresentation of the Bostonians, on the whole they had no great grievance. The fact that the *Public Advertiser* printed their letter as soon as the exigencies of communication would permit, is evidence in point.[2]

While the repeal of the Stamp Act was being agitated, the hand of the merchant and manufacturer could be very plainly seen. They suffered from the measure. But there is comparatively little evidence in the papers during the Townshend Acts agitation that these classes felt seriously affected. Of course English merchants and manufacturers were concerned with anything that might injure the American trade, but during most of the period workingmen were well employed and prices for manufactured goods were high.[3] The Bristol merchants, who

[1] *P. A.*, June 8, 1770.

[2] Preston's letter was in *L. C.*, April 23, 1774.

[3] "A Merchant" claimed manufactures were flourishing, *Gaz.*, Feb. 5, 1770, but was sharply answered by "Another Merchant", *Gaz.*, Feb. 7, 1770.

had a very large American trade, seem to have been the most concerned, for early in 1769 they instructed their parliamentary representatives to be "strenously active in obtaining a repeal of the Laws, imposing duties on British manufactures exported to America" which had been "found *highly* prejudicial to the nation in *general*, and to this city *in particular*."[1]   Early in 1770, on finding that orders to their merchants, conditional upon the repeal of the acts, amounted to £200,000, they agreed to request Matthew Brickdale, one of their members in Parliament, to do his utmost "in obtaining a repeal of the said acts."[2]   At about the same time they drew up a petition to the king in which they charged that the Acts had ruined their manufactures.[3]   "The Colonist's Advocate" ridiculed the idea that the non-importation measures did not hurt; else why should British merchants be so agitated, why were there so many idle ships in the river?[4]   When the repeal was pending, it was reported that about twenty ships would leave for America a week after it had been accomplished and that great numbers would depart before the month was up.[5]   A year after the repeal it was alleged that some two million pounds worth of goods had been exported.[6]   Merchants and manufacturers, then, did feel the effect of the American measures, but they were by no means active in agitating for repeal.

[1] *L. C.*, March 14, 1769.

[2] *Univ. Mag.*, Feb., 1770, p. 105. For another mention of conditional orders see *P. A.*, Jan. 30, 1770; *Lloyd's E. P.*, Jan. 29, June 24, 1770.

[3] See *P. A.*, Jan. 6, 1770; *S. J. C.*, Jan. 6, 1770.

[4] *P. A.*, Feb. 19, 1770. He was answering arguments made by "Old Mentor;" see *P. A.*, Jan. 9, 18, 1770, and other letters; see *P. A.*, July 18, 1770.

[5] *P. A.*, Feb. 22, 1770; see a contradictory paragraph March 14, 1770.

[6] *P. A.*, May 20, 1771.

A contemporary explanation of their inactivity was that, " The Russian War has caused so great a Demand for several Branches of our Manufactures, which used to be in Demand for America, that the Manufacturers have not felt the Want of the American Trade so severely as they otherwise would have felt it, . . ." [1]

Petitions by the voters of Middlesex [2] and by the Livery of London, [3] though called forth primarily by the Wilkes disputes and the arbitrary nature of the reign, did not fail to mention that similar complaints could be made in the case of the colonies. These petitions mentioned America only incidentally, and the argument was more constitutional than commercial. The petitions were similar. A paragraph from the petition of the London Livery shows the support given to the American viewpoint. " They have established numberless unconstitutional regulations and taxations in our colonies. They have caused a revenue to be raised in some of them by prerogative. They have appointed Civil-law Judges to try revenue causes, and to be paid from out of the condemnation money." This sympathy was due not to commercial reasons but to the fact that some Englishmen thought England and America had a " Common Cause."

As 1770 wore on, the repeal of the hated acts began to

[1] *P. A.*, July 26, 1770.

[2] See *Gent. Mag.*, June, 1769, pp. 289-292; see *L. C.*, June 6, 1769.

[3] See *Univ. Mag.*, Supp., vol. xxiv, 1769, pp. 375-6, and *Town and Country Mag.*, July, 1769, p. 350. In the 15th and 16th centuries the guilds, mysteries, fraternities or livery companies, so called from their special gowns or livery, were the chief governing element in London. After that time their power declined and by 1770, though made up of influential citizens, their corporate power was but a shadow of what it had been. They still exist; see G. Unwin, *The Guilds and Companies of London* (1908) and W. C. Hazlitt, *The Livery Companies of the City of London* (1892).

loom as a possibility. For some time frequent hints had
been appearing in the papers.[1] The determination of the
ministry to retain the tax on tea left English shippers to
America, commercial agents and many others at a loss
to know what to do, for they were by no means certain
the Americans would receive any goods unless the repeal
was total.[2] The papers were chary of reporting the vote
of March 5, in the House of Commons, which took off
all duties lately imposed " except the additional duties on
a certain Asiatic Herb." To ward off prosecution, probably, the act was reported in this manner: " Bets, last
Night, on Colony Affairs, we are told were

For the Colonists	240
Against	142
Majority	98 "[3]

These "odds" were the votes in the decisive action of
March 5.

Not very much attention was taken of the repeal, however. That it had long been foreshadowed may have
been one reason and that the repeal was eminently satis-
factory to common-sense commercial instincts, another.
Perhaps more important was the fact that Wilkes had
come to the front again. On April 12, 1770, the acts
were officially repealed, except the tax on tea. Then the
papers felt free to comment, but in that same week
Wilkes was released from prison. Agitation in his behalf had begun before that, for on March 14 a petition
presented to the king in his interests had been "con-
temptuously dismissed."[4] With the opening of a purely

[1] See *Gaz.*, May 20 and 23, 1769. Three letters May 23.
[2] *P. A.*, March 12, 1770.
[3] *S. J. C.*, March 6, 1770; see *P. L.* and *Gaz.*, March 7, 1770.
[4] See article on Wilkes in *Dic. Nat. Bio.*

domestic problem of such magnitude, American affairs were crowded into the background.

Authentic news of the partial repeal reached America early in May; by the middle of June the American reception of the repeal began to receive comment in the English papers. The Americans at once began to debate among themselves whether to resume importation of all articles except tea, on which the duty still remained, or whether to continue non-importation of everything as a protest against the tea-tax. Boston took the latter stand[1] and, various other colonies, it was reported, would take the same step.[2] On July 9, the merchants of New York decided to import all goods except tea.[3] The papers reported that New York's action was dependent, however, on agreement by Boston and Philadelphia,[4] and that these towns were holding out for complete non-importation. The differences in American sentiment, it was thought, would henceforth prevent the non-importation movement from being prejudicial to England.[5] The English took keen interest in the breaking down of the movement in America; but it did not become the topic of the day. In September the *St. James's Chronicle* reported, "Bets of eight to three were laid last Night in the City, that the Bostonians would import before the End of the next Month."[6] In November and December reports were printed that the Bostonians, the most stubborn opponents of the Townshend Acts, had agreed to import all articles except tea, and the Townshend Acts

[1] *S. J. C.,* June 19, 1770.

[2] *P. A.,* July 20 and Sept. 10, 1770.

[3] Schlesinger, *Colonial Merchants,* pp. 226-227.

[4] *P. A.,* July 25, 27, 1770.

[5] *P. A.,* July 28, Nov. 12, 1770.

[6] *S. J. C.,* Sept. 20, 1770.

dropped out of the English papers, though the evil they had done lived on.[1]

In October, when it was already becoming apparent that the non-importation agreements were to be abandoned, "An Old Correspondent" took a final fierce shot at the Americans by insisting that their movement had been one of crookedness and shady dealings from the start. He alleged it had been a big farce, as the New Yorkers had learned before withdrawing. Hancock and others, he said, had had full stocks when they proposed it, and held to non-importation just as long as these stocks lasted, and then, while giving the mechanic class of Boston the idea that they were living up to the agreements faithfully, imported secretly.[2]

[1] *S. J. C.*, Nov. 20, 1770; *London Mag.*, Dec., 1770, p. 640.
[2] *P. A.*, Oct. 20, 1770; see an answering letter, *ibid.*, Nov. 3, 1770.

CHAPTER VIII

Tea and the Punishment of Boston

After the repeal of the Townshend Acts, almost nothing, with one exception, was printed concerning America until the Boston Tea Party and resultant measures once more focussed the attention of the press on the colonial problem.[1] The one exception was the discussion of letters written by Hutchinson and other crown officials in America to Thomas Whately, which showed that native Americans had proposed and solicited many of the measures considered most grievous by the colonists.[2] By some unknown means Franklin had secured these letters and sent them to America, where, contrary to a pledge, they were published. On both sides of the Atlantic they caused a great stir, but in England it was mainly incidental to the American question. No one, at first, knew how these confidential letters had gone to America. In consequence accusations were made, and the honor of William Whately, brother of Thomas, and of John Temple, who had had access to the letters, having become involved, the two fought a duel in which Whately was

---

[1] This lack of interest was not reflected in the papers alone. " During the whole year of 1771, and the following years, no debate on any matter connected with that question is reported in the Parliamentary history of England. The Historical Summary in the 'Annual Register' for 1773 gives to America less than a single column of printed matter. In the Historical Summary for 1775 American affairs fill a hundred and forty-two out of a hundred and fifty-eight pages." Trevelyan, *American Revolution* (New York, 1899-1912), vol. i, p. 139.

[2] A good discussion and bibliography on this discussion is in Howard, *op. cit.*, p. 260 *et seq.*

wounded. Over the question of honor and the duel, rather than over the letters themselves or their import, a sharp controversy raged in the *Public Advertiser* and other papers. Franklin finally put an end to the controversy by writing to the *Public Advertiser* that he alone was responsible for sending them to America. "A Member of Parliament" thought the publication of the letters would improve matters since, " The subtle spies, the secret traitors (i. e. the writers of the letters) stand now confest. . . . The Americans are fully satisfied, that the severe measures of this country arose from these misinformations; which, joined with a conviction of our having been imposed upon, has produced a mutual turn to reconciliation." [1] These sentiments are so similar to some expressed by Franklin that he may have inspired or perhaps written them himself.[2]

This led to the famous examination of Franklin before a committee of the privy council. The occasion of the meeting was the presentation of a petition from the assembly of Massachusetts asking for the removal of Hutchinson and Oliver, but Solicitor General Wedderburne used the opportunity for launching a severe personal attack upon Franklin. Most of the newspaper accounts were sympathetic to Franklin, a typical one reporting that Wedderburne pronounced "a most severe Phillipic on the celebrated American philosopher, in which he loaded him with all the *licensed* scurrility of the bar, and decked his harangue with the choicest flowers of Billingsgate." [3] The dismissal of Franklin from his office as deputy postmaster-general immediately followed, and he resigned his agency for Massachusetts. Upon both of these actions most of the comment was favorable

---

[1] *P. A.,* Nov. 25, 1773.

[2] See Franklin's *Works* (Spark's ed.), vol. iv, p. 412.

[3] *L. P.,* Feb. 2, 1774; also in *M. J. & E. A.,* Feb. 3, 1774.

to Franklin.[1] Another incident, during these years of comparative calm, was the attack on the Gaspee. ·It was reported, but received little comment.[2]

To reopen the American question was to irritate an old sore. Englishmen were so painfully aware of it. that many of them had developed decided opinions. Not that strong opinions regarding the refractory colonists had been lacking before, but now colonial troubles had begun really to rankle. As the friends of the administration revealed growing bitterness, the patriots, or popular party, became more pronounced in their expressions of friendliness toward their oppressed brethren beyond the Atlantic. This result arose in part because the situation now began to justify stronger language on either side, and in part because much of the American argument pro and con had become entangled in, and was a sideplay to, domestic politics. America had become a standing partisan issue, and there is nothing to indicate that eighteenth-century politicians lacked much zeal in using such issues.

The singling out of Boston and Bostonians as the chief malcontents in America was also more noticeable after 1773. The Bostonians were charged with being the ring-leaders; they were " without exception, the most turbulent of any on the Continent "; they were " bigots of the most dangerous kind." [3] ·Many were satisfied that the trouble would

[1] See *M. J. & E. A.*, Feb. 1, 3, 8, 17, 1774; *Lloyd's E. P.*, Feb. 9, 1774; *L. P.*, Feb. 25, March 30, 1774; *P. A.*, Jan. 24, 1775; *P. L.*, Feb. 26, 1774; *Gaz.*, Feb. 16, 1774. Smyth, in Franklin's *Writings*, vol. x, p. 266 says that from Jan. 11 to Jan. 29 Franklin was denounced in the press. There is little comment on Franklin of any kind during this period. Just after the examination a fair amount is found but it is mostly pro-Franklin. In 1775 Franklin was occasionally denounced, but rarely earlier; see *P. A.*, March 15, 17, 22, 1775.

[2] *K. G.*, July 21, 1772; *Gent. Mag.*, Aug., 1772, p. 389; *Lloyd's E. P.*, July 20, 1772.

[3] *M. J. & E. A.*, Sept. 3, 1773; *Lloyd's E. P.*. April 4, 1774.

have been settled long since but for factious, turbulent Boston.

The first news of the Boston Tea Party, a reprint from the Boston *Evening Post* account of February 20, 1773, was printed January 20, 1774.[1] Before that time tea had figured slightly in the news. Notice had been taken of American attempts to find substitutes for tea; criticism had been made, at the time of the partial repeal of the Townshend Acts, that the tax on tea had not been dropped also; and the poor financial condition of the East India Company had not escaped mention.[2] Some plans were made to relieve this distress by increasing the drinking of tea,[3] the loss of the American market was noted, and the exportation of tea to America with a tax still on it was considered by some " as one of the most critical enterprises " the company had ever engaged in, for no one could be sure that the Americans would " buy at all." [4] During the month before the reception of the tea news in England, frequent accounts of the American attitude toward the importation of tea reveal an apprehension that trouble might result.[5]

Within a few days after the first news of the incident was published, all the English papers had reported the riotous behavior of the Bostonians. The Tea Party is commonly considered the last straw, the incident which finally caused the English government, backed by an almost solid popular resentment, to take stern and decisive measures against the Bostonians. Trevelyan speaks of the " heat and unanimity " of the people and says, "The country was in a

[1] *London E. P.*, Jan. 20, 1774.

[2] See *Gent. Mag.*, Jan., 1773, pp. 20, 40-41; *K. G.*, Jan. 30, 1773; *L. C.*, July 6, 1773.

[3] *Gent. Mag.*, Feb., 1773, pp. 59-60; *Lloyd's E. P.*, Feb. 1, 1773.

[4] *L. P.*, Sept. 3, 1773; see *M. C.*, Jan. 13, 1774

[5] See *L. P.*, Jan. 5, 21, 1773, Dec. 1, 13, 31, 1773.

temper for any folly which its rulers would allow it to commit;" while Bancroft says, " The press roused the national pride, till the zeal of the English people for maintaining English supremacy became equal to the passion of the ministry." [1] There can be no doubt that the government was moved by the Tea Party incident to take harsh measures, but the papers of the time give no evidence of anything like a unanimous demand by an indignant and enraged English public that the Americans be brought to condign punishment for the insult.

A *Middlesex Journal* paragraph of the same issue that carried the report, demanded the punishment of Boston and urged that any other course of conduct would be " an infamous instance of servile pusillanimity," [2] but this was far from the overwhelming sentiment. It might be balanced by a *London Packet* paragraph, in the same issue which first told of the troubles, stating that the resistance of the Americans reflected " equal honor on the spirit and understanding of the Colonists " as such resistance was against action best described as "tyrannic." [3] "Lycurgus," apparently with tea in mind, though he made no mention of it, styled the action of Boston, seditious, turbulent and insolent; [4] but a *London Packet* contributor thought the Boston action showed that the " Ministers, or rather that miserable Cabinet Junto in whom *only* the King thinks proper to confide, are as cordially despised in America as they are detested in England," and continuing said, " The passion for power on one side, and the resolution to preserve liberty on the other, give a

[1] Trevelyan, *American Revolution* (New York and London, 1899-1912), vol. i, p. 154; Bancroft, *Hist. of the U. S.* (New York, 1882), vol. iii, pp. 470-471, 472 respectively; see Channing, *Hist. of U. S.*, vol. iii, p. 133.

[2] *M. J. & E. A.*, Jan. 22, 1774.

[3] *L. P.*, Jan. 21, 1774.

[4] *M. J. & E. A.*, Jan. 25, 1774.

very serious . . . a very dreadful complexion to this dispute."[1] "A Constant Reader" saw humor in the situation. He said the acts of the ministry had been cobbling. "And to complete the cobling, tea is sent to America to make soup for the fish. Is not this cobling? Political cobling with a vengeance. Ha! Ha! Ha!"[2] One grim humorist wrote that some Scotchmen were going to America, whence they were going to send the East India Company "a Cargoe of American Scalps, as some Recompence for their Tea."[3] Another reported that the bayonet was going to be used against the Americans, but that in spite of all "it is known that the glorious sons of America will sing Tea-Deum."[4] A noble lord, however, thought the best punishment would be to, "Hang, draw, and quarter fifty of them,"[5] while a paragrapher thought that peace and good order would be restored, "If government would hang about one hundred of these puritanical rebels in Boston."[6] In the fall of 1774, a sarcastic friend of the ministry said that when the blessed babes of Boston robbed the tea ships "every *good* Englishman . . . . extolled the rebels to the skies, and the newspapers celebrated the virtue of the action."[7]

Other statements by friend and foe could be quoted to the same effect. There was evidence that the ministry was greatly irritated, but the newspaper comment on the matter pro and con was not great: there was no sign of a great, united, popular burst of feeling. The incident which looms

---

[1] *L. P.*, Jan. 31, 1774; also in *London E. P.*, Jan. 29 and *M. C.*, Jan. 31, 1774.

[2] *Town and Country Mag.*, Jan., 1774, p. 24.

[3] *S. J. C.*, Jan. 26, 1775.

[4] *L. P.*, Feb. 28, 1774.

[5] *M. J. & E. A.*, Jan. 27, 1774.

[6] *M. J. & E. A.*, March 12, 1774.

[7] *K. G.*, Oct. 26, 1774; also in *G. E. P.*, July 26, 1774.

so large in American minds received surprisingly little comment in the contemporaneous papers. Although the *London Chronicle,* sometimes called a Tory paper, reported the Tea Party on January 22, it printed nothing but a few rather non-committal items on tea the rest of the month. Its reports of the trouble consisted of a number of extracts from American papers, and it published little that originated in England. During the whole month of February following, no letter writer felt moved to let *London Chronicle* readers know his opinion of the Americans, and even the paragraphs printed were colorless. On March 2 the same paper printed the following paragraph, which was the strongest opinion thus far printed in its columns. " It is now generally understood that the most spirited and coercive measures will be taken by the Mother Country, to bring back her refractory children to a proper sense of their duty, and the common interests of the whole empire." A short and unsigned letter, the first referring to the American troubles, printed in this paper, appeared March 15. It was bitter and sarcastic against the Americans, but though it undoubtedly referred to the Tea Party it did not mention tea. It was followed shortly afterwards by a letter signed " Junius Americanus," the signature used by Arthur Lee. Throughout March the interest increased, not because of the Tea Party itself but because Parliament was beginning to consider what punishment should be meted out to the Bostonians.

The action Parliament might take in the case interested every partisan politician, whatever he might think of the right or wrong of the Bostonian affair. Continuing through April in the *London Chronicle,* the interest grew as Parliament debated the punishment. Even in that paper almost as much pro-American sentiment as anti-American was printed in the first three months after England knew of the outrage, and in general this is true of the other papers and magazines. Not until the punishment of Boston became a political issue did the Boston Tea Party cause very much discussion, and at no time did the papers indicate a greater unanimity regarding the American question than at other periods.

It was very clear that there was a wide divergence of opinion concerning the Boston Port Bill. "A Friend to the Rights of Mankind" wrote that, in listening attentively to the various sentiments, he had found the Americans "applauded and condemned with equal injustice."[1] A paragrapher lamented that Englishmen were indifferent in regard to America or even approved her acts, and urged that all should be "unanimity here to support the pillars of the constitution."[2] "Marvel," a frequent writer on the American side, asserted that the "nation in general" was on the side of the Americans.[3] The "moderate and sensible" part of the people were said to see no possible advantage in being severe against them.[4] Opinion was divided as sharply as it ever had been; in fact the chief result of the tea destruction was to intensify rather than to change the sentiment seen in the papers. The intensification did not take place at once, however, but only when the provisions of the Boston Port Bill came to be generally known.

One important sign of the division of opinion was that soon after the Tea Party the first items in regard to the unpopularity of military service began to appear in the papers. A *London Packet* paragraph stated "there is great doubt but army and navy in general will refuse acting with

[1] *M. J. & E. A.*, Feb. 24, 1774.

[2] *M. J. & E. A.*, March 8, 1774; see *M. C.*, Feb. 23, 1774, for a letter by "Clericus."

[3] *L. P.*, March 14, 1774.

[4] *M. J. & E. A.*, March 8, 1774.

alacrity against the Americans." [1] It was also reported that the command of the ships sent to America had been offered to several gentlemen " all of whom *unaccountably* declined that *honour*." [2] What opinion lurks in the italics? Officers were reported to have declared that service against the Americans was " quite repugnant to their feelings as men and Englishmen." [3] Later, reports of reluctance on the part of both officers and men became common, but it is noteworthy that the first of such reports appeared just after the tea-destroying activities of the Bostonians. In this period it was also very commonly reported that the military effectiveness of the forces in America was very seriously affected by desertions. A paragrapher said, " The soldiers are so caressed in America that they desert daily. ' Who would fardels bear,' that could have land for nothing, peace, plenty, and a fine country." [4] The import of these reports was that the military subjugation of America would be a difficult matter, a theme frequently stressed. [5]

As at the other periods of trouble trade items telling of the value of American commerce began to appear. Those who advocated the severe punishment of Boston were invited to consider " that America is a *Hen* that lays her *Golden Eggs* for Britain; and that she must be cherished and supported as part of the great family of Britain." [6] Others reminded readers that British merchants had upwards of four millions of property in America, referring to debts owing to them, and that this would be the first sacrifice in

[1] *L. P.*, March 11, 1774.

[2] *L. P.*, April 1, 1774; *K. G.*, April 6, 1774.

[3] *M. J. & E. A.*, April 9, 1774; *M. C.*, April 9, 1774; see *M. J. & E. A.*, April 19, 1774; *K. G.*, Aug. 31, 1774, April 13, 1774, Feb. 18, 1775.

[4] *M. C.*, Aug. 9, 1774; see *M. C.*, Aug. 30, 31, Sept. 3, 6, 10, 29, 1774.

[5] *L. P.*, Feb. 9, 11, 14, 16, 1774.

[6] *S. J. C.*, March 31, 1774.

case of hostilities. In addition more than one hundred thousand artificers were said to gain their daily bread from the same trade.[1] It was widely reported that the merchants trading to America were so anxious for conciliation that they offered Lord North £19,000, the value currently put upon the destroyed tea, if he would postpone action against Boston until the Massachusetts Assembly met. North was alleged to have replied that the matter was now before Parliament and must be allowed to take its course.[2] A querist wanted to know if it was thus wise to disregard the wishes of those very people whose property was so deeply concerned.[3] The *London Magazine* printed much about the proposed punishment, "As the Boston Port Bill is of vast importance to the mercantile part of the nation, and indeed to the whole British Empire."[4] The merchants at "Bristol, Manchester, and Liverpool" were early reported to feel bad effects from it.[5]

By the middle of March the debate over the punishment of Boston was on in full swing. Opponents of the American viewpoint were wont to refer to the fact that property had been destroyed by the turbulent colonists and without compensation for the damage. Even the friends of America regretted that the tea had not been paid for, as this fact gave their opponents an argument difficult to meet.[6]

There was some complaint in the newspapers that Mr. William Bollan, the agent for Massachusetts, had not been heard in the House of Commons. According to one paragraph, "The refusal of the House of Commons to hear Mr.

---

[1] *S. J. C.,* March 15, 1774; see *Lloyd's E. P.,* March 14, 1774.

[2] *K. G.,* March 23, 1774.

[3] *M. J. & E. A.,* March 22, 1774.

[4] *London Mag.,* April, 1774, p. 165.

[5] *M. J. & E. A.,* April 16, June 14, 1774.

[6] See *K. G.,* Nov. 16, 1774; *L. C.,* Aug. 13, Nov. 12, 1774.

Bollan is loudly condemned as unconstitutional; as it is positively asserted, that he had a right to be heard, which they could not legally deny him." [1]

Schlesinger has stressed the proposition that the colonial merchants, rather than the general public, instigated and encouraged the American resistance to the importation of tea, not because they objected to taxation but because they foresaw the ruin of their tea trade. The new regulations would enable the East India Company to undersell even their smuggled tea. As efforts to protect their business were not likely to gain enthusiastic popular support, the merchants agreed among themselves to emphasize the taxation issue involved, thus hoping to gain popular approval of their opposition to the importation of tea, although their real object was to protect their own economic interests. [2] There is evidence that this explanation of the tea trouble had some acceptance in England, but the great majority of writers treated the question as one of taxation or sovereignty. To most anti-American writers the question was, as "Periander" phrased it, "whether the colonies shall rise superior to the mother country, or whether the mother country shall retain any farther dominion over the colonies?" [3] One paragrapher said it was "whether the *right* of taxation, be Here, or *there?*" [4]

A few Englishmen, but not many, were moved to complain of the monopoly which the arrangement gave to the East India Company. " Pompilius " asserted that Lord North had achieved a great stroke of policy in making the

---

[1] *M. J. & E. A.*, April 28, 1774; see *S. J. C.*, April 30, 1774; *L. P.*, May 4, 1774; *K. G.*, May 4, 1774.

[2] Schlesinger, *Colonial Merchants*, p. 264.

[3] *P. A.*, March 10, 1774; also in *G. E. P.*, March 12, 1774; see *G. E. P.*, May 7, June 4, 1774.

[4] *Jackson's Oxford Journal*, Jan. 29. 1774.

arrangement as he foresaw the event and thus took steps to insure East India Company support in the ensuing struggle, for by that "means only they could form a probable hope of reimbursement." [1]   "Mercator" thought it amazing that no public writer had objected to the arrangement " on the grounds of Monopoly, which it certainly is, . . ." and wondered the merchants trading to America did not remonstrate against such proceedings.[2]   "A Dealer in Tea" and " Y. Z." both protested that the power given to the company would ruin them and other independent tea dealers in England,[3] but they made no mention of its effects on merchants in America.

" Old Mentor " assured the public that most of the objections in America were made by "American Dutch smugglers." [4]   A Gloucester Journal paragraph said American objections apparently arose from the duty, " but the real state of the case " was that this clamor was " entirely raised against the tea by a set of crafty men," who carried on " a great smuggling trade with Holland in that article; and should the English tea be admitted at this low duty, the smuggling trade would be rendered of little value." [5]   An unsigned letter in the Middlesex Journal made a similar charge with great plausibility, concluding that the American troubles were " first set on foot by the American smugglers, and then blown into rebellion by the preachers." [6]   However, as has been noted, such explanations of the trouble were not common.

[1] L. P., Dec. 26, 1774.

[2] M. C., March 21, 1774.

[3] M. C., April 28, P. A., May 20, 1774 respectively.

[4] Gaz., Feb. 24, 1770.

[5] Gloucester Journal, Jan. 24, 1774.

[6] M. J. & E. A., July 25, 1775.

The chief objection to the punishment itself was that it made no distinction between the innocent and the guilty. The Tea Party was declared to have been the work of a few; therefore only a few should be punished.[1] The real offenders would scarcely be affected at all by the Boston Port Bill while thousands of innocent persons would be brought face to face with hardship and misery. Others objected that the contemplated action was entirely too heavy for the offence. These were fond of referring to the treatment meted out to the rebels of 1745 and comparing the gravity of their offence and the lightness of their punishment with the lightness of the crime and the heaviness of the penalties in the case of Boston.[2] In part this was simply a way of showing the prevailing anti-Scotch animosity, but in large part it was inspired by real sympathy for the Americans.

There was some debate concerning the mood the punishment would produce in the colonies. Some held it would kindle all America until the different colonies would make common cause with their oppressed brethren.[3] The common administration view was that the Bostonians, though enraged at first, before long would come to terms because they would not be supported by the other colonies; and as soon as New York and Pennsylvania began to take the Boston trade, the recalcitrant New-Englanders would begin to see a light.[4] In August, when the coercive measures against Boston were causing the ardor of some of her merchants to cool, a number of newspaper items mentioned the

[1] *M. C.,* May 2, 1774.

[2] *K. G.,* April 2, 13, 1774; *L. C.,* April 12, 1774; *P. A.,* April 8, 1774.

[3] *M. J. & E. A.,* April 12, 1774; see *M. C.,* March 22, April 9, 1774; *K. G.,* April 13, 1774; *L. P.,* March 16, 21, June 8, July 13, 1774.

[4] *Lloyd's E. P..* April 25, 1774; see *P. A.,* June 17, 1774; *L. C.,* Nov. 11, 21, 1775.

dissensions in Boston. It was reported that the "land-holders and tradesmen are divided against the merchants, the latter of whom are for healing measures, but each pro-testing against the proceedings of the other." [1] It was said that many duels occasioned by these dissensions had been fought in Boston. [2]

On all but one of the measures taken by Parliament just after the destruction of the tea, the debate waxed back and forth without a preponderance of opinion on one side or the other. Pro-American arguments, certainly, were not less common than at other periods.

On the Quebec Act, however, opinion was overwhelm-ingly against the administration. At no time during the American disputes did any single measure have such a pre-ponderance of sentiment. An abstract of the proposed bill appeared in the *London Chronicle*, May 7, 1774, but not until the publication of another abstract on June 11, 1774, did newspaper discussion of it become prominent. The paragraphers called it "infamous and despotic," [3] "the boldest stride to despotism . . . . made by any set of men since the restoration." [4] Lord North, they said, positively denied that the act "was a child of his"; and it was called a "base, tyrannical bastard." [5] The newspapers were never able to give a father to the bill since no one was so bold as to claim it. It was declared to make "G——e the T——d of E——d, ten thousand times more despotic than Lewis

---

[1] *K. G.*, Aug. 6, 1774; *Newcastle Chr.*, Aug. 13, 1774; *M. J. & E. A.*, Aug. 4, 1774; see *M. J. & E. A.*, Aug. 13, 1774; see *L. C.*, Sept. 29, 1774; *P. A.*, June 17, 18, 1774.

[2] *L. P.*, Aug. 29, 1774.

[3] *K. G.*, June 1, 1774.

[4] *M. J. & E. A.*, May 31, 1774; see also May 28, 1774.

[5] See *M. J. & E. A.*, May 31, Aug. 27, 1774.

the XV was, when he ruled that kingdom with a rod of iron." [1]

The bill was said to be "universally objected to; " [2] the populace were reported to have acted rudely when his majesty appeared in public, shouting at him, "No popery, no French Government," and similar expressions. [3]   Bets were reported at five to four that the Bostonian and Quebec Bills "turn out the ministry before Michaelmas Day next, and Five to One, War or no War, that they are routed on or before the first of January 1775." [4]   The names of those who voted for it were circulated everywhere and it was predicted that the next general election would "determine whether the Pope or the Voice of the people" was "to chuse a British Parliament." [5]   The Society of the Bill of Rights undertook to send the names of those who had voted for and against it to every county and borough of the kingdom. [6]   All those who had voted for it were reported to be under suspicion.

Even before the Quebec Bill, "Pacificus" gave as his belief that the "general Opinion of the People of England" regarded the measures taken against the Bostonians as "unjust and oppressive, as well as senseless and impolitic." [7] After the Quebec Bill a paragrapher reported, "There never was a time when the citizens of London so universally inclined to the patriotic side. The late unpopular American acts have totally sunk the ministry in the esteem of all ranks

[1] *K. G.,* June 1, 1774; see *K. G.,* June 25; *L. P.,* June 13, 1774; *S. J. C.,* May 19, Sept. 1, 1774.

[2] *L. P.,* June 8, 1774.

[3] *S. J. C.,* June 23, 1774.

[4] *S. J. C.,* June 14, 1774.

[5] *S. J. C.,* July 2, 1774; see *M. J. & E. A.,* June 16, Aug. 6, 1774.

[6] *S. J. C.,* Aug. 27, 1774; see *Univ. Mag.,* May, 1775.

[7] *S. J. C.,* May 21, 1774.

of the people that wish well to their country," [1] and " P. C. D." asserted, " The Judgement of the Publick upon the Measures of Government has never been, within my Memory, more general, more uniform, nor, perhaps, more in the Right " than upon the Quebec Bill.[2] Certainly the newspaper expressions had never been more uniform on any measure of the pre-revolutionary period.

The three most common objections to the bill were embodied in "The humb'l Petition of the Lord Mayor, Aldermen and Commons of the City of London in Commoncouncil assembled." [3] The first objection advanced was that the Quebec Bill substituted French for English law in all civil cases, and took away trial by jury. Second, they objected because by it the Roman Catholic religion would be the only established religion; and, third, because it established arbitrary power in that all legislators were appointed at the pleasure of the crown, and otherwise totally subverted the constitution. A fourth objection, often advanced, though not in this petition, was that the bill intended to erect a Catholic Quebec that would be a cudgel with which to threaten the Americans.[4]

On the first three counts the press echoed with the indignation of angry and excited Englishmen. Trial by jury was pronounced the greatest right of Britons, and its abolition " too scandalous a Clause to have been framed by any Englishman." [5] The outcry against that part of the act was great but it was a mere whisper beside the objections to the sections favoring the Catholics.

[1] *M. J. & E. A.*, Oct. 1, 1774.

[2] *S. J. C.*, July 9, 1774.

[3] *Univ. Mag.*, June, 1774, and widely printed in other publications.

[4] *Gloucester Journal*, June 13, 1774.

[5] *S. J. C.*, June 23, 1774; see *L. P.*, June 8, 17, 1774; *M. J. & E. A.*, Aug. 13, 1774.

Mr. Mascall, speaking before five hundred freeholders of Middlesex, was reported to have said that he recognized in the bill " the old prostitute, the whore of Babylon," and he styled the premier, " the butcher of a minister." [1] Many other expressions as strong were printed. The politicians of Westminster made political capital of the issue and pledged themselves to obtain relief. Lord Mahon told the electors he would work to obtain the repeal of the Quebec Act by which " Popery, arbitrary power and French laws " were established in so great a part of the empire.[2] The famous Wilkes and John Glyn, in a joint announcement, promised to work for a repeal of it and of all the measures against Boston,[3] and a paragraph stated that Westminster voters made the promise to work for the repeal a *sine qua non* to election.[4] A common humorous report had it that Lord North was not afraid to go through with the bill because he had " got an absolution for it." [5] A Popish army, it was reported, was to be raised in Quebec, and this step was denounced as illegal.[6]

Some comment was caused by the fact that the boundaries of Quebec were so greatly enlarged by the act " as to almost surround " the other colonies; and it was said that Quebec, as constituted by it, was larger than all the other colonies combined.[7] This was done intentionally, said one paragraph, for as Canada covered New England on the north and west, the Popish subjects in it were well fitted to form a " Corps de Reserve " to reduce the Bostonians.[8]

[1] *L. C.* and *M. J. & E. A.*, Sept. 27, 1774.

[2] *K. G.*, Sept. 21, 1774.

[3] *K. G.*, Oct. 1, 1774.

[4] *K. G.*, Oct. 8, 1774.

[5] *M. J. & E. A.*, June 30, 1774.

[6] *L. C.*, Sept. 10, 1774.

[7] *L. C.*, July 16, 1774; see *L. P.*, June 10, 1774; *K. G.*, July 23, 1774.

[8] *S. J. C.*, Nov. 8, 1774 *passim*.

The argument was common that Quebec was held as a cudgel over the Americans. " Let the Yankies beware of a back stroke!" wrote " The Political Annotator." [1] "A Fellow Countryman " charged the avowed purpose of the act was to use Roman Catholics " to awe, if not to imbrue their hands in the blood of British Protestant subjects." [2]

One friend to the manufacturers pointed out the danger to British exports from such an extension of the territories of Quebec. His argument was that this would prevent the opening up to settlement of any new rich lands. This would cause a congestion of population in the regions already settled, and the speedy settling of all cheap, available land. This policy, he said, was ruinous, because as long as Americans had cheap lands they would not manufacture, but as soon as lands became expensive they would turn to industrial pursuits. The matter, he urged, should be considered carefully. Five letters in the *Middlesex Journal*, three signed " Crito " and the other two probably by the same man, all argued in the same vein. [3]

Though the overwhelming bulk of the arguments were against the Quebec Act, it should not be inferred that none defended it; for though none could be found to father the bill, some could be found to fight for it. " Poor Old England " defended it on the broad grounds that, circumstances being different in Canada, especially as to religion but also as to nationality and customs of the inhabitants, the bill, which would have been unjust in England and in other parts of the empire, was eminently just there. [4] Others defended it on the ground of toleration. " Publicola " asked, " And

[1] *P. A.*, Jan. 21, 1775; *L. C.*, Jan. 21, 1775.

[2] *L. C.*, Feb. 11, 1775; see *K. G.*, Dec. 14, 1774; *L. P.*, Dec. 23, 1774; *S. J. C.*, May 31, 1774.

[3] See *M. J. & E. A.*, June 21, 23, 25, 28 and July 5, 1774.

[4] *K. G.*, June 25, 1774.

were the Ministry then to adopt the very worst principle of
Popery, To persecute the Canadians into Protestantism?" [1]
" G " argued that the new regulations were not only just,
as they fitted the inhabitants, who were used to French laws,
but also entirely consistent with the articles of capitulation
made between Lord Townshend and Count Ramtzey, in
1759, and were thus carrying out the sacred faith of national
treaties.[2] "Columbus" said those who thought the bill was
aimed against the Bostonians were wrong, for it had been
in agitation for years and actually had been framed many
months prior to the time when the Boston Port Bill could
possibly have been heard of. In spite of this, he complained, the people insisted that it was designed to get the
aid of the Canadians against the other colonists.[3]

Impartial students quickly admit that in the main the bill
was just, and that defenders of the kind just mentioned
were in the right. A letter by "P. C. D.," previously mentioned, gives the real reason for the outcry. "The People,"
said he, " are too much interested in Events of this Tendency to let them pass with an insolent Shrug of the Shoul-
ders," and " A Stroke of this Kind, aimed at the Religion
and Liberties of our Country, must awaken the most drowsy
Slumberer among us." [4] A favorite theme for letter writers
during the whole pre-revolutionary period was alarm at the
" progress of Popery." In short, the Quebec Bill touched
the English people on an easily aroused set of prejudices,
their religious prejudices, and called into play one of their
fiercest passions. The other measures had perhaps violated
their constitution, but, if so, the violations were at a distance of three thousand miles. The Quebec Act, however,

[1] *L. C.*, Jan. 3, 1775.
[2] *L. C.*, July 21, 1774.
[3] *P. A.*, Jan. 9, 1775.
[4] *S. J. C.*, July 9, 1774.

had certainly granted favors to Catholics, and though those Catholics were beyond the seas, Englishmen were keenly aware of Catholics in England, of whose power and position they were constantly suspicious. Many bitter struggles had England had over religion, and many slumbering animosities survived. The Quebec Bill gave occasion for the enemies of Catholicism in England to fan these animosities to a fiery heat. Englishmen at home were much more moved by hatred of Roman Catholics than by any feeling of sympathy for the Americans. Thus the pro-American sentiment over the Quebec Act was rather intolerant and illiberal toward Roman Catholicism than friendly or liberal toward America.

Although the ministry quickly decided that punishment should be meted out to the Bostonians, this action did not stop the English newspapers from filling their columns with letters and paragraphs of protest. American sentiment, after coercive measures had been decided upon, was very strong. It was reported that in " most of the towns in the north of England . . . the people unanimously murmur about the measures putting into execution against the Americans. . . ." [1] "An Honest Man," a strong anti-American writer, declared that the advocates of America were many, but were moved " by interest, popularity, or disgust against the Ministry." If he is to be taken at his word the American side was then the popular one. Continuing, he asserted that they " sounded forth their speeches in every News Paper " in the kingdom.[2]

A charge " Candidus " made with great force was that the war measures against the Americans were the work of a "despotic junto," which had disregarded all advice, " the voice of the people," " public clamour " and " national ex-

[1] *L. P.*, June 17, 1774; *M. C.*, June 16, 1774.
[2] *Lloyd's E. P.*, Sept. 19, 1774.

pediency," until an unnatural appeal to the sword was being made to give the decision.[1] It was observed that, " the Question rightly understood, is not Great Britain against America, but the Ministry against both." [2] Although the administration was careful to combat this assertion, it was frequently repeated.[3]

Non-importation came in for a share of attention, but the argument over it was not very warm. Those who maintained that non-importation was not dangerous as it was unenforceable by the Americans, had the upper hand. General agreement seemed to be with "The Political Annotator," who, taking note of the common report that the New York merchants would not cooperate with Boston, asserted cynically that "To suppose that any people will keep an *agreement* which *interest* prompts or *necessity* urges them to break, is an absurdity truly patriotic." [4]

As the year 1774 waned, however, it became apparent that, whether American non-importation was successful or not, the manufacturers of England were suffering from a decline of trade.[5] Paragraphs began to appear telling that the chief manufacturing towns of England were about to petition to have the American acts repealed; [6] soon the battle of petitions was on, the majority of them pro-American. During January, 1775, these petitions from the manufacturers and merchants were the chief topics discussed in the press. One administration paragraph sought to discredit the

[1] *K. G.*, Nov. 9, 5, 13, 1774; see *Univ. Mag.*, Supp., 1774, p. 363 *et seq.*

[2] *S. J. C.*, Jan. 26, 1775; see *P. A.*, Aug. 9, Nov. 9, 1774; *American Archives*, vol. ii, pp. 1607 and 1617.

[3] *S. J. C.*, Jan. 5, 1775; *G. E. P.*, March 10, 1774.

[4] *P. A.*, Jan. 2, 1775; see *L. C.*, Jan. 3, April 22, 1775; *P. A.*, Jan. 26, 1775.

[5] *S. J. C.*, Nov. 22, Dec. 20, 1774, Jan. 7, 1775; *L. C.*, Jan. 5, 17, 19, 28, Feb. 16, May 18, 1775.

[6] *Lloyd's E. P.*, Dec. 21, 1774; *P. A.*, Jan. 7, 1775.

action of the merchants who " became a cat's paw for the American rebels at the repeal of the Stamp Act," and had " humbly submitted to be handled in the same contemptible manner by the Bostonian monkeys twice since." [1]   "Britannicus," who thought it was only from the " landed gentry, whose all depends on the fate of this island," that the English nation " was to hope for any safety," argued that merchants were not to interfere in this affair, as their views were too partial.[2]   The merchants were admonished, were assured that they were mistaken, and were freely charged with petitioning under pressure from colonial merchants, who were threatening to refuse payment of their debts unless English merchants bestirred themselves in behalf of the Americans.   Some said the merchants really wanted to enforce American obedience but were afraid to let it be known because of this non-payment threat.[3]

The most-talked-of petition of the period was the one from Birmingham.   It was called the " most extraordinary petition," " the so much talked of," and it otherwise attracted unusual attention.   This petition stated, "That your petitioners are apprehensive, that any relaxation in the execution of the laws respecting the Colonies of Great Britain, will ultimately tend to the injury of the Commerce of this Town and Neighbourhood." [4]   They therefore prayed that the measures taken against the Bostonians be strictly enforced.[5]   This was not long in drawing fire from the friends

[1] M. C., Feb. 11, 1775.

[2] P. A., Jan. 26, 1775; see L. C., March 2, 1775.

[3] See L. C., Jan. 7, 12, 31, 1775; P. A., April 2, 1774; K. G., Feb. 1, 1775; G. E. P., Jan. 7, 10, 12, 1775; M. J. & E. A., April 22, 1775; L. P., Feb. 8, 1775; L. C., Sept. 17, 1774; Gent. Mag., July, 1774, p. 333; Gloucester Journal, Aug. 29, 1774; S. J. C., Aug. 16, 1774.

[4] L. P., Feb. 3, 1775.

[5] A counter letter of thanks was sent to Burke, signed by merchants who said they had a " principle share in the American trade." London E. P., Feb. 16, 1775.

of America. " No Hypocrit " addressed a letter " To the English Hollanders; or Birmingham Knaves," charging the Birmingham petitioners wished to involve America in a war so they could then be engaged " in making Stands of Arms for both Parties," which they were then secretly doing " by Way of Holland and Germany for one." [1] This last referred to a common charge that Birmingham manufacturers were supplying arms to America by way of Holland.[2] Numerous writers waxed indignant against the petitioners, who were represented to be but greedy sellers of munitions eager to reap a fortune off the horrors of a fearful civil war. A newspaper rhymster dedicated a poem to the people of Birmingham, two stanzas of which follow:

"You petition'd the King, against Liberty, truth,
  And pray did you do it to show your great care?
  (Alas! 'tis a pity you open'd your mouth,)
  For alas! its contents were but Birmingham ware!

· · · · · · ·

" Since you pray'd our good Monarch to cut all their throats,
  And plunge them at once in a sea of despair;
  I suppose as he kindly attended your votes
  The arms that you sent them were Birmingham ware." [3]

In the middle of February it was reported that Lord North was about to bring in a bill to confine colonial trade to Great Britain, Ireland and the British West Indies, and to prohibit the Americans " from fishing on the banks of Newfoundland, and other places. . . ." [4] This speedily brought forth remonstrances from the Lord Mayor, Aldermen, and Livery of the City of London,[5] London mer-

[1] *S. J. C.,* Jan. 28, 1775; see *London E. P.,* Feb. 9, 1775.
[2] *S. J. C.,* March 22, 1774; *L. P.,* April 26, 1775.
[3] *L. P.,* April 26, 1775; see *P. A.,* Jan. 26, 28, 1775.
[4] *L. C.,* Feb. 18, 1775.
[5] *Gent. Mag.,* April, 1775; see *Gent. Mag.,* and *London Mag.,* Feb. and March, 1775.

chants [1] and others who were fearful of injury to trading interests. The remonstrants not only condemned the most recent measures against the Americans, but they criticized the whole course of action against the colonies. The West India merchants also petitioned against the prohibition of the Newfoundland fishing on the ground that their trade would be very seriously cramped by it,[2] for much of their sugar and molasses were traded to the New Englanders for Newfoundland fish. A great deal of attention was given at this time to a Quaker petition on the matter.[3]

The friends of the Americans counted much on the Quakers. Dr. Fothergill and David Barclay, who were much in consultation with Franklin, were trying to influence the ministry to reconciliation in 1774 and 1775,[4] and England watched their efforts with great interest. The ministry was reported to be greatly alarmed at their action, and to be trying to buy them off; but both England and America were praying for their steadfastness, as it rested " with them to absolutely save their country." If the Quakers stood firm it would have more effect than " all the things yet written or said for America. . . ." [5] "Attakullakulla " addressed the Quakers in fervent terms and mixed metaphor when he asked them to shake off their lethargy and step forth the saviors of America after he had taken the mask from off the minister's face and showed "the serpent with the damned cloven foot." [6] Many paragraphs asserted that England and America would both be saved if only the Quakers would

[1] See *L. C.,* March 14, 16, 18, 28, 1775.

[2] *L. C.,* Feb. 14, 1775; see *M. J. & E. A.,* May 30, 1774, March 21, 1775.

[3] *L. C.,* March 18, 21, 1775; see *M. J. & E. A.,* April 23, 1774.

[4] Sharpless, *The Quakers in the Revolution* (Philadelphia, 1899), pp. 110-116; see 4 *Am. Archives,* vol. ii, p. 181 *et seq.*; *Dic. Nat. Bio.*

[5] *K. G.,* April 30, 1774; *L. P.,* April 27, 1774.

[6] *L. P.,* May 4, 1774.

stand firm.[1]   The clue to Quaker power seems to be given
by a paragraph which stated that a combination of the
Quakers would be very distressing to the minister, " as they
hold great sums of money in our Funds, and are in possession of most of the ready cash that circulates among the
colonies." [2]

It was during this period also that many politicians standing for office took pains to state that they were for measures
of conciliation with America.   It is noteworthy that these
vote catchers thought it wise to take that side.   Not a single
one of the many political advertisements of the general election took the stand that America should be punished.   "Opifex " was astonished " that it should be the most essential
qualification in a Member of the British House of Commons, to weaken the hands of Government, and strengthen
the Colonist's resistance." [3]   Though advocacy of America's
cause does not seem to have been a plank of the greatest
popularity, the absence of anti-American planks has some
significance.

A copy of the Boston Port Bill reached that city May 10
and soon set the colonists to thinking of concerted measures
of remonstrance and resistance.   Opinion was not long in
crystallizing for a general congress; and, on September 5,
1774, the First Continental Congress began its work at
Philadelphia.   Beginning in August the English showed in-
tense interest in the forthcoming meeting, for it was generally
expected to prove dangerous to English interests.   One paragraph said the government would prevent it as " unconstitutional and illegal." [4]   The writer of another wanted to know

[1] L. P., May 4, April 22, 29, 1774; K. G., Nov. 23, 1774; L. C., March
18, 21, 1775; Gent. Mag., March, 1775.

[2] L. P., Nov. 21, 1774.

[3] G. E. P., Oct. 22, 1774.

[4] Lloyd's E. P., Aug. 5, 1774 passim.

if there was a statute " which deems such meetings illegal." [1]
The writer of a letter, *"On the intended congress in America,"* was sure it augured ill for England, as it was nothing
but an act of resistance and tended toward a union of the
colonies, whereas the true policy of England was to keep
them as "divided, as separate and unconnected as possible."
Once a union was formed they would be obedient no longer.
He wanted to know if there was not some way to declare
all persons who took part in it " guilty of high treason." [2]
One paragraph expressed the belief that the congress would
accomplish much good, but most of the comments were
either hostile or non-committal. [3]

The various state papers of the congress, all widely
printed in England, caused a great stir.   They were applauded and censured in about the same measure as the
other American acts.   A widely-copied paragraph said, "The
People in Power now affect to blame one another; they cry
they could not think the Americans would have acted so
stoutly. . . ." [4]   Dr. Johnson wrote his famous pamphlet,
Taxation No Tyranny, the subtitle of which was, *An Answer to the Resolutions and Address of the American Congress,* against them.   This was the most-commented-upon
pamphlet of the whole pre-revolutionary era, and storms of
abuse and scurrility, much of it personal, mingled with some
praise, were directed at its author.   "Numa," the great at-
tacker of the congress, issued letter after letter in the *Public
Advertiser.*

[1] *M. J. & E. A.,* Aug. 30, 1774.

[2] *M. J. & E. A.,* Aug. 25, 1774.

[3] *M. J. & E. A.,* Sept. 13, 1774; *ibid.,* Dec. 22, 1774, Sept. 27, 1774, Aug.
22, 1775; *Lloyd's E. P.,* Oct. 24, Dec. 14, 16, 19, 21, 26, 1774; *P. A.,*
Dec. 21, 26, 1774, Jan. 2, March 15, 18, 1775; *London E. P.,* Jan. 19,
1775; *L. C.,* Feb. 9, May 16, June 24, 1775.

[4] *P. A.,* Dec. 19, 1774.

CHAPTER IX

Concord, Lexington and Bunker Hill

The possibility of war in the colonies early occurred to the letter writers. In 1774 and in 1775, before the first actual fighting, this possibility was mentioned more frequently. Some assured the public that the approaching war would be won with ease by the British, for a few miserable colonists could never stand against the power that had humbled France and Spain. It would not be necessary to use an army, the fleet alone could subdue the chief American cities and bring the colonists to their knees.[1] Others insisted the war should not be entered into lightly, as the nature of the country was such that the Americans, who would prove no mean foes, would be able to make a stout resistance, if not to win outright.[2] The military prowess of the Americans, their marksmanship and their skill in forest fighting were often mentioned.[3]

Thus the English public was not unprepared for the news of Lexington and Concord, which was first published in their papers May 29, 1775. The earliest account was an American one, taken from the *Essex Gazette* of Salem, Massachusetts, which, of course, gave the American version of

[1] *L. C.*, Jan. 21, 28, 31, 1775; *L. P.*, Nov. 23, 25, 1774; *L. C.*, Nov. 24, 1774; *S. J. C.*, Dec. 22, 1774.

[2] *L. P.*, March 14, 1774; *S. J. C.*, Dec. 24, 1774; *L. C.*, April 22, 1775. This debate did not stop with Concord and Lexington. For subsequent warning that the war would be difficult see *K. G.*, June 14, 1775; *L. P.*, Aug. 2, 1775; *M. J. & E. A.*, June 10, 1775, *passim.*

[3] *M. J. & E. A.*, April 8, 25, June 3, July 13, 1775.

the affair. This had a long start over the official report, which did not appear until June 10. During the intervening days it was freely charged that the government was concealing news from America, and the tools of administration were reported to be representing the engagement as "meer fiction."[1] The *Public Advertiser* announced it was "desired by Authority to request the Public would suspend their Judgement upon that Event until they can be more authentically informed of the Particulars."[2] Speculative persons were puzzled to account for the slowness of the administration.[3] The American side was given a still more favorable report on May 31 by the printing of affidavits by Simon Winship, James Barret and Edward Thoroton Gould, and signed statements by other Americans.[4]

When the official report first came out in the *London Gazette,* a government organ, much more of a bulletin than a newspaper, at once the differences between it and the American account were noted. An effort was made by both American and British sympathizers to fix the guilt of firing first on the other side, though some, as "Opifex," wrote that it made very little difference as the Americans had committed acts of hostility long before.[5] The *London Magazine,* friendly to the Americans as usual, printed the official and the American versions for purposes of comparison, and was much inclined to give more credence to the accuracy of the latter.[6] Both sides knew the propaganda value of good

---

[1] *P. A.,* June 9, 1775.

[2] *P. A.,* May 30, 1775; see a letter by Arthur Lee, May 31, 1775.

[3] *S. J. C.,* June 10, 1775; see 4 *Am. Archives,* vol. ii, pp. 870-871.

[4] *P. A.,* May 31, 1775. A paragraph in the *P. A.,* Aug. 1, 1775 said Gould had repudiated his affidavit.

[5] *L. C.,* June 20, 1775.

[6] *London Mag.,* June, 1775, p. 323. Almost the same in *Univ. Mag.,* June, 1775, pp. 331-333.

atrocities, and the Americans were accused of scalping and cutting the ears off the wounded; but these tales were dismissed lightly by the *London Magazine,* which said it was well known that savages existed among the politest peoples.[1]

The reverberations from Concord and Lexington had not had time to die out when the fateful news from Bunker Hill once more directed all attention to America. The printers, by this time, had been long expecting news of serious armed conflict; in fact, nearly all of them published a false report of an engagement alleged to have taken place on June 23.[2] Rumors were rife. This time, however, the administration was first with the true report, which made its initial appearance in the *London Gazette* of July 25, 1775. The papers quickly had this and other accounts and the battle was soon well reported. If there had been any doubts that the sword was to be the arbiter, these doubts now vanished. The war of words was to cease; the war of bullets and death was to begin.

The reader, living in our present nationalistic age, when patriotic feeling may sweep like wildfire over a country, and when freedom of speech and of the press are severely curtailed at the beginning of hostilities, will think: now certainly there will be a unanimity of opinion in the papers, now there will be no more expressions of sympathy for the Americans. Especially those who remember something of the change in expressed opinion in America when war was declared against Germany in 1917 and know something of what happened abroad in 1914, will expect that an outbreak of hostilities on such a scale would put an end to the expression of pro-American sentiment in the papers. Such,

[1] *London Mag.,* June, 1775, p. 323; see *P. A.,* June 13, July 8, 1775; *S. J. C.,* June 24, 1775.

[2] See *P. A., P. L., W. E. P.* for July 25, 1775; *Lloyd's E. P.,* July 26, 1775.

however, was not the case. The friends of administration did assert that " Unanimity now prevails," but it was a hollow assertion. " A Friend to Truth," taking note of such a remark, sharply disagreed. He stated that having been for some time in the country, he did not know about London, but in the country the case was just the opposite, as " by far the major Part of the People, that I have conversed with, are very friendly to the Americans, and view them as an injured People." He also related that he had an account from a gentleman in Devonshire that the people there, as well as in Cornwall, " were strongly biassed in Favour of the Americans." [1] "A North Briton" said that the Americans had the constitutional side of the dispute so that " it need be no wonder that the greatest part of the nation are ardent in wishing success to the Americans, and in deprecating the arms employed by their Sovereign." [2] The London papers give the impression that these remarks were true. The *London Evening Post* especially was well filled with expressions of American sentiment. It is certain that as large a proportion of American sentiment was printed after the conflict as before, and it was more decided in tone. Concord, Lexington and Bunker Hill, it would seem, were hailed almost with a note of exultation. The reasons for this are probably many, but two considerations may have borne especially upon the situation. First, the idea of the state as the goal, the ultimate aim, the highest conception of human organization had not secured anything like the popular acceptance it has today. The conception by which the nation state, absolute, and infallible,[3] has been elevated to become a veritable God, had not yet been evolved and

[1] *P. A.,* Aug. 18, 1775.

[2] *M. J. & E. A.,* June 29, 1775.

[3] " ... there is nothing higher than it in the world's history." Bernhardi, *Germany and the Next War,* translated by A. H. Powles, p. 46.

proclaimed by men like Bernhardi, much less found acceptance in millions of minds. Second, this war was in truth,
as the English were continually saying, a civil war. Not
merely a civil war between two territorial divisions of the
empire, but essentially one between two schools of English
thinking, whose differences are most conveniently seen in
those diverse opinions of traditional Whigs and traditional
Tories. The reader should not think that all men called
Whigs in 1775 were pro-American, for some of the most
objectionable measures taken against the colonies were taken
by men wearing the Whig label. The Americans, however,
in large part, seemed to have the traditional Whig view in the
struggle; and hence they shared traditional Whig sympathy.

" Numa," a prominent anti-American writer, railed bit-
terly at the spirit displayed in the papers. His bitterness
perhaps led him to overstatement, but that he had grounds
for his complaint every reader of the papers must admit.
He told of the delight at the civil war, of the expectation
and hope of the patriots that the troops sent to America
would be cut to pieces, and declared that the sooner the contest ended the better :

As our Newspapers deem it public Spirit, to encourage the
Traitors beyond the Atlantic . . . and as every Man is represented an Enemy to the Constitution who ventures to breathe
a Syllable in Behalf of this unfortunate Country: As Subscriptions are collected by open Advertisement in the very
Capital, for the avowed Purpose of aiding Rebellion.[1]

He could not too severely censure the papers for their attitude. " Curius Dentatus," another administration writer,
told that, " Every Token of Satisfaction the Heart " could
" express was displayed by these Men [the patriots] upon
the *Report,* magnifying into a *Defeat* of his Majesty's
Troops, a Skirmish between a Detachment of them, and the

[1] *P. A.,* June 17, 1775; see *P. A.,* July 8, Aug. 12, 1775.

deluded Colonists. . . ." [1]   An administration paragraph
declared, "The Bostonians are now the favourites of all the
people of good hearts, and weak heads in the kingdom.
Their saint-like account of the skirmish at Concord, has
been read with avidity . . . believed and rejoiced in." [2]
The implication was that most of the heads were weak.   A
paragraph reported, "The prevailing toast in every company
of true Englishmen is, ' Victory to the Americans, and re-
establishment to the British constitution.' " [3]   An indignant
correspondent in the *London Chronicle* complained of the
attitude of the newspapers.   According to him, " Were a
man to judge of the times by the complexion of the daily
publications in the newspapers, he might consider this country as on the very brink of destruction."   The acts and
prowess of the Americans, he said, were praised and exaggerated out of all proportion, and their heroism was mag-
nified while the English were stigmatized with the " appel-
lation of poltroons, villains, and scoundrels." [4]   A correspondent in the *London Chronicle,* however, consoled himself
by remarking that, since the great majority of substantial
men favored administration, " the wretched instruments of
faction " might " be safely permitted to keep possession of
the newspapers." [5]   As far as may be judged from the
papers, the news brought the English people more joy than
sorrow or anger.[6]

[1] *P. A.,* June 26, 1775; see July 6, 1775.

[2] *L. P.,* June 7, 1775; also in *M. C.,* June 7, 1775; see an opposing paragraph, *M. C.,* July 19, 1775.

[3] *London E. P.,* Aug. 15, 1775.

[4] *L. C.,* July 1, 1775.

[5] *L. C.,* Nov. 4, 1775.

[6] See 4 *Am. Arch.,* vol. ii, p. 870 for a letter stating that the news of
Concord gave very great pleasure in England " as the newspapers will
testify " and that pro-American sentiment was increased " particularly
since the above intelligence."

Previous to the initial conflicts it had been the practice of some, or as a paragraph had it, " the fashion at St. James's to despise the Americans, to call them Cowards, Poltroons, etc. . . ."; to represent them as men who would run at the first sight of a British regular.[1] Now appeared a number of paragraphs telling of the bravery of the Americans and of their determination not to submit. The paragraphers and letter writers, recalling the derogatory and boastful remarks of some of the politicians, got considerable fun out of calling attention to the difference between the prophesied cowardice and the realized bravery. " William Tell " waxed sardonic over the statement in Gage's report of Bunker Hill, that the action had " shewn the Superiority of the King's Troops." Superiority over whom? he asked. Over superior numbers of French or Spanish regulars?

No Sir, of the Americans—Of the Americans! What, of those dastardly, hypocritical Cowards, who, (Lord Sandwich knows) do not *feel bold* enough to dare look a Soldier in the Face! Of those undisciplined and spiritless Yankies, who were to be driven from one end of the Continent to another with a single Regiment![2] What, of those skulking Assassins, who can only fire from a Distance from behind Stone Walls and Hedges! Good God, Sir . . . . "

More ridicule followed in the same ironical vein.[3] "Camillus," in a letter of exuberant exaltation, thought the period arrived " which must convince the *libidinous Catch-singer,* that the Americans are not those dastardly Wretches that he would have them believed: Will he now think it an easy Matter to dragoon the Inhabitants of a vast Continent,

---

[1] *London E. P.,* April 15, 1775; see *L. C.,* Jan. 7, 10, 1775; *K. G.,* Jan. 18, 1775; *Gent. Mag.,* Jan., 1775, p. 45.

[2] Referring to an alleged statement by Amherst that with 5000 men he would engage to march from end to end of the colonies; see *Newcastle Chr.,* April 22, 1775; *London E. P.,* April 15, May 25, 1775.

[3] *P. A.,* July 31, 1775; also in *London E. P.,* Aug. 1, 1775.

. . . ." [1] The English accounts all agreed that the Americans had behaved with bravery at Bunker Hill, and the weight of the opinion inclined the same way in regard to Concord and Lexington.

In the period just after hostilities began, Putnam was the best known of the American commanders, and numerous tales of his prowess and ingenuity were circulated. At last "Anti-Americanus" broke out, " I can keep my temper no longer. . . . Whatever company I have been in for these three weeks past, I have heard nothing but the praises of General Putnam. Putnam will do this, Putnam will do that, Putnam will do everything." [2] An anecdote concerning him had the following interesting heading: " Anecdote of the brave General Putnam who is now the boast [*sic*] of every table where men dare be honest in these putrid times." [3]

Enemies of Lord North took advantage of the situation to launch some very harsh attacks upon him. His conduct was reported to have been one of " incredible Absurdity," and his system of politics was styled " paltry, shallow, contemptible." " B." declared that North and his junto had " taken more pains to make them rebels than is necessary to make rebels good subjects." The Americans had asked for nothing, he said, except to be put in the same situation they were in before the last war.[4] Political strife and dissatisfaction ran so high that one paragrapher announced that " Betts " had been laid that if the American question was not settled before winter there would be " Civil War and Revolution in England before the Spring." [5]

[1] *P. A.*, July 29, 1775; see letter by " Cassandra," perhaps Dean Tucker, Aug. 10, 1775 and a letter by " Harlequin " in the *L. C.*, Sept. 5, 1775.

[2] *K. G.*, Aug. 16, 1775.

[3] *L. P.*, Aug. 2, 1775; see *L. C.*, June 13, July 8, 15, 1775; *K. G.*, June 3, Sept. 30, 1775; *G. E. P.* and *M. J. & E. A.*, June 10, 1775.

[4] *Gent. Mag.*, July, 1775, p. 325; see *S. J. C.*, June 6, Aug. 10, 1775.

[5] *P. A.*, July 8, 1775.

The Lord Mayor, Aldermen, and Commons of the City of London drew up a humble petition and address to the king praying his benign attention toward the distractions of the Americans. Lamenting the measures that had driven the Americans to "acts of desperation," they prayed that the recent harsh acts against them might be suspended.[1] This petition and the answer of the king were both widely printed in the papers. At a meeting of the Livery of London in the Guildhall, a petition was drawn up to the king which asserted that if the rights of the Americans were invaded they ought to resist such invasion and that the resistance was their "indispensible duty to God."[2]

The friends of administration who had long since taken note of the large body of supporters of the American cause in England, now attacked them with a greater energy. These patriots, as they were called, were declared to be the "principal dependence" of the Americans in the war just started; without their encouragement, it was asserted, the Americans never would have dared to raise their heads.[3] James de Solis, who was decidedly anti-American, said it had been justly observed that dissensions in England had "added spirit to the cause of the Americans," and complained "that almost one half of England" had given "their voices against their own country."[4] The colony advocates were reported to be trying to convince the people of England that a great majority of the English were in favor of the Americans, but they were challenged to give any proof.[5] "P. Q." explained the pro-American sentiment by asserting,

---

[1] *Universal Mag.*, July, 1775, p. 45.   Printed in several publications.

[2] *Univ. Mag.*, July, 1775, p. 44.

[3] *L. C.*, June 13, 1775; *L. P.*, June 9, 1775; *London E. P.*, Aug. 8, 1775; *M. C.*, June 9, 1775.

[4] *L. C.*, Feb. 4, 1775; see *L. P.*, Jan. 18, 1775.

[5] *L. C.*, Oct. 31, 1775; see Nov. 2, 1775.

"It is very certain that one disaffected person makes more clamour than fifty loyal subjects." [1] " Silanus," a strongly anti-American writer, declared that the Americans at Concord and Lexington were first given rum to spirit them up to resistance, but that failed. They were finally persuaded to fight by the report that 60,000 citizens of London had taken up arms for them. [2] Another account had it that they fought only when they were assured that there were risings all over England and that Wilkes, Lord Mayor of London, had risen against the government and was encamped on Blackheath, with 80,000 men. [3] The ministry, for their part, were reported to attribute the resistance of the colonists entirely to the speeches of Chatham, Camden, Burke, Barré, Saville, and " also to the newspapers." [4] Alderman Harley claimed that every falsehood had been employed to make the people of America think that the people of England would join them, and that their belief in the imminence of English support was the cause of their resistance. Alderman Sawbridge, citing the famous Dr. Rush as his authority, asserted that the Americans did not think they had much support in England, but on the contrary, supposed a very great majority of Englishmen were against them. [5]

As the quarrel became more and more inflamed the aiders and abettors of America were not content with expressions of sympathy alone but showed their approval of the Americans in more substantial ways. [6] The same number of the

---

[1] *Lloyd's E. P.,* Aug. 14, 1775.

[2] *L. C.,* July 13, 1775; see *L. C.,* July 18, Aug. 15, Sept. 21, Oct. 26, 1775.

[3] *Gloucester Journal,* July 10, 1775.

[4] *L. P.,* July 12, 1775; see *K. G.,* July 4, 1775.

[5] *L. C.,* July 8, 1775; see *K. G.,* July 4, 1775; *L. C.,* Nov. 25, 28, 1775.

[6] Subscriptions for the relief of suffering in Boston were taken before this. *Jackson's Oxford Journal* reported on Jan. 7, that upwards of 10,000 pounds had been sent to Boston in the preceding three months;

Middlesex Journal, that first reported Concord, had a paragraph saying, "Very large subscriptions are now commenced in the city for the use of the Bostonians. Two patriotic Aldermen subscribed yesterday £50 each." [1] On June 2, at a meeting of the Constitutional Society,[2] that body voted that a subscription be started for the relief of the widows, orphans and parents of those beloved Americans who, " preferring death to slavery, were, for that reason only, inhumanly murdered by the King's troops at or near Lexington and Concord. . . ." According to the newspaper account, the sum was immediately collected and sent to Dr. Franklin.[3]

Ever since the beginning of the trouble with America some Englishmen had declared that the cause of America was also the cause of England, that the Americans were fighting the battles of England as well as their own.[4] Three

L. C., Feb. 23 said upwards of 3,000 pounds had been privately raised and sent; *Newcastle Chron.,* Feb. 25 said 15,000 pounds were raised in less than half an hour at a meeting of London merchants. On the same subject see *L. C.,* Feb. 11, 1775; *L. P.,* Feb. 13, March 8, 22, 1775; *K. G.,* Dec. 28, 1774, Feb. 15, 1775, March 22, 1775; *Gloucester Journal,* March 20, 1775; *London E. P.,* Dec. 24, 1774.

[1] *M. J. & E. A.,* May 30, 1775; *K. G.,* June 3, 1775.

[2] This was an offshoot of the Society of the Bill of Rights. This latter society was founded in 1769 to support John Wilkes. Arthur Lee tells about its early membership in one of his letters; see R. H. Lee, *Life of Arthur Lee,* p. 28; see *D. N. B.,* under Tooke, who was a prime mover in it. In 1771 Tooke and Wilkes had a quarrel and a minority withdrew with Tooke and formed " the Constitutional Society, which was to carry on the agitation without any regard to Wilkes' private interests."

[3] *L. P.,* June 9, 1775; *K. G.,* June 14, 1775. Apropos of this the *D. N. B.* account under Tooke says, " No notice was immediately taken, but in 1776 some of the printers of the newspapers were fined, and in the next year Horne was himself tried before Lord Mansfield (4 July, 1777). . . . " He was convicted and judgment finally confirmed; see *L. C.,* Feb. 18, 1775.

[4] See *London E. P.,* June 28, Dec. 20, 1774; *Adam's Weekly Courant,* Jan. 10, 1775.

letters from contributors to the Boston fund spoke of the common cause.[1] "H. B. T." sending ten pounds for Boston relief said, "Their cause is the cause of England," and added that he had as many thousands as he now sent pounds if they were needed.[2] These men were not silent after hostilities began. A commonly printed paragraph proclaimed that there was " nothing left for the welfare of this country, but the virtue and fortitude of America."[3] If the colonists stood firm all would be well, but if they yielded, the liberties of both countries would be destroyed.[4] "Raleigh" quoted with approval the words of an English friend, uttered upon receipt of the news of Concord, " Happy Britons, if they shall owe the revival of their liberty to the success of their American brethren."[5] The Livery of London in an address to the electors of Great Britain made the statement that the cause was common.[6] John Wilkes announced that he felt it his duty equally to oppose the oppressors of his fellow men on either side of the Atlantic.[7] It was reported that an association was forming in London to support the Americans, as, "The brave, wise and free citizens of London will never sit still, and quietly suffer the ruinous and arbitrary measures of the Ministry respecting America to be executed."[8]

The resignation of Lord Effingham on April 12, 1775, was the most conspicuous of the resignations of British officers on account of unwillingness to serve in a war against

---

[1] L. P., March 8, 1775.   They are in 4 Am. Arch., vol. ii, pp. 54-55.

[2] L. P., Feb. 22, 1775.

[3] K. G., April 26, June 14, 1775; London E. P., June 10, 1775.

[4] See Newcastle Chr., June 17, 24, 1775.

[5] L. C., June 13, 1775.

[6] L. C., Sept. 30, 1775.

[7] L. C., Nov. 4, 1775.

[8] London E. P., June 15, 1775.

the Americans. Although the resignation was submitted in April, the papers did not print the letter in which he justified his action until September.[1] His step was known before that, however, for on June 24 he was publicly thanked by the Livery of London[2] and later by citizens of various cities, including Dublin, Newcastle and Southwark. Far more praise than censure of his action was printed. Reports of resignations and threatened resignations of other officers were frequent.

It was freely predicted that soldiers sent to America would desert in large numbers. As early as September, 1774, reports had been printed that " on account of the desertion of troops in North America," the ministry was considering using Hanoverians.[3] From time to time paragraphs told that they could be obtained in sufficient numbers if there should be any demand for them. After hostilities had begun, comment upon the policy of using such troops began to be printed. Not only Hanoverians but also Hessians,[4] Swiss[5] and Russians[6] were mentioned as possibilities. Generally the reports had it that these troops would be sent to Ireland, or to Gibraltar, or would be kept at home as reserves, but occasionally the rumors were that they were to be sent to America. Their employment was generally un-

---

[1] *London Mag.*, Sept. 1775, p. 456. Widely printed.

[2] *Univ. Mag.*, July, 1775, p. 45.

[3] *M. J. & E. A.*, Sept. 3, 1774. In August items in this paper about desertion of troops in America were common; see *L. P.*, Aug. 31, 1774.

[4] *L. C.*, Dec. 20, 1774; see Aug. 10, Sept. 12, Oct. 21, 1775. A *M. J. & E. A.* letter, June 8, 1775, said the little German princes were in high spirits at the prospect of hiring troops to England.

[5] *K. G.*, Dec. 6, 1775.

[6] *K. G.*, Aug. 26, Sept. 20, 1775; *L. C.*, Oct. 12, 1775. The Russian troops were reported to be in return for services to the Russians in their war with the Turks.

popular; Englishmen recalled that foreign mercenaries had been employed in the last two wars and spoke against them.[1]

The need for such troops was imperative because of the very great difficulty the recruiting parties had in getting men to enlist for the war. "An Englishman" declared that fewer than 200 English army recruits had been enlisted in three months, despite the ministerial reports to the contrary, and that sailors were likewise difficult to get.[2]   Like the officers, the men found the prospect of service in America very disagreeable. If the war had been against France or Spain, said the reports, great numbers of men could have been obtained but service against the Americans was a different matter.[3]   Recruiting parties in the country were reported to be meeting with no success,[4] and the necessity of hiring Hessians, to which the ministry was ultimately reduced, is evidence that there was much truth in the assertions.

That divisions in England and the friendliness to the Americans after the hostilities had actually begun were very considerable is shown by the note of joy in the newspaper sentiment over the American successes in the opening conflicts.   The strong efforts of the ministerial writers to discredit pro-American opinion in themselves is evidence that the opposition was very powerful.   Such volleys of letters and paragraphs were not fired at a phantom.   They were fired at a very real and substantial sympathy with America, and the volume of the fire testifies to the strength of that sympathy.   Much of the pro-American sentiment, of course,

---

[1] L. C., Nov. 9, 14, 1775; K. G., Sept. 6, 1775; P. A., June 20, 1775 (favorable to employment of Hessians), June 26, 1775 (an answer); see June 28, 1775.

[2] London E. P., Aug. 17, 1775.

[3] L. P., Aug. 4, 1775; see "An Old Soldier" M. C., March 14, 1775.

[4] L. P., Aug. 18, 14, 1775; see K. G., April 15, June 3, Sept. 9, Nov. 15, 1775.

was the result of partisan politics. Much of it was primarily the opposition of the " outs " to the " ins ". But a very great deal of it was motivated by a more disinterested sympathy for America. The subscriptions for America, the reiteration that the cause of America was common to England, the resignation of officers, and the impossibility of recruiting sufficient troops in England to fight against the Americans, all go to show how strong was the opposition to the American measures of the government.

CHAPTER X

Conclusion

THE revolutionary period may be conveniently and naturally divided into two sections: the preliminaries of the revolution and the war of the revolution. In America the first period may be said to have ended in July, 1775, when Washington took command of the Continental Army. In England the chronology of the two periods is almost the same, for the first period may be said to have ended August 23, 1775, with the issuance by the king of the "Proclamation for Suppressing Rebellion and Sedition." In this proclamation the king declared that the Americans were in a state of rebellion and that aiders and abettors of this rebellion would be guilty of treason. It is at this point that this study is brought to a conclusion. The preliminaries of the revolution were now over and the war had begun. A study of the English press during the period of hostilities has promise of high interest, but it does not come within the scope of this investigation.

A significant aspect of this study has been to make evident the great amount of support the American viewpoint found in the English press. Some attempt to account for it and to sum it up surely will not be idle. At the first mention of hostilities, the present-day American, with his conventional ideas of American history, is given a fresh viewpoint when he finds that the English, contemplating war in America, spoke of it as a civil war. Civil war it certainly was, but Americans after a century and a half of separate political existence, do not usually think of it in that light. They call it the War of the Revolution, and then forget the significance of the word " revolution." Americans know, of course, that the colonies were once in the same governmental system with England but the terms " civil war " and " revolutionary war " carry connotations so different that they rarely think of our American Revolution as civil strife.

That it was a civil war not merely in regard to territory but also because of the fact that it was between two schools of thinking, both of which were found in England, is evidenced by the frequent use of the " common cause " argument, to which allusion has been made. Recent students of revolutionary history have demonstrated that the struggle was a civil war in the colonies likewise, for probably a third of all the people and more than a third of the educated classes were Loyalists in America.[1] The position these Loyalists took and the arguments they used often had close similarity to those used by the court party in England. The Americans who were not Loyalists were either indifferent or were Patriots; and in England we find a sympathetic party also called Patriots. In many respects these English Patriots and these American Patriots had a similar political tradition, the Whig tradition and a similar outlook. From the common law of England and from England's body of great tradition they had developed political theories with many likenesses. Only, in America, the freedom of a new land without shackling traditions, the pioneer life on the frontier of civilization, the democratizing influence of the wilderness, had caused these theories to develop faster than in England. Yet, in England, they were far from dead.

Thus it came about in England that the administration and the opposition both spoke of the war as a civil war, altho perhaps the two parties did not interpret the phrase exactly alike.

[1] Tyler, *Loyalists in the Am. Rev.*, Am. Hist. Rev., vol. i, p. 31; McLaughlin, *Confederation and Constitution*, pp. 37-38.

The administration looked upon the conflict as a rebellion against the constituted authorities, a conflict between the Americans and the British government. The opposition may have looked upon the conflict as this and more, for to many of them it meant a conflict between ideals of government, and still further, a conflict between the traditions of the " Glorious " Revolution and an increasing and ever more oppressive tyranny supported by the prevailing corruption. Lulled by inertia and corruption, Britain was fast succumbing to a growing tyranny. The English friends of the American cause alleged that while English nerves were dulled and their senses calloused, in America the tradition of freedom burned brightly, for the Americans were neither enervated nor decadent. Their passion for liberty, their sensitiveness to encroachments on their freedom had not been overcome by a flood of corruption. This was in the eighteenth century, the age when admiration of the " noble savage " had become almost a cult, when the virtues of primitive peoples and customs were being preached, when George III delighted to call himself " Farmer " George. The Americans, fresh from contact with mother nature and unspoiled by a corrupting civilization, were taking the lead in resisting encroachments upon liberty. It was well for England, thought many. If once tyranny prevailed in America, it would be but a short step before its work would be accomplished in England. Then English liberties would be no more.

Thus we have Englishmen, such as " Laconick," praising the Americans, and asking, " Are not we then degenerate to the last degree in despairing of supporting the constitution against the encroachments of the C——? " [1]   A paragraph declared that Englishmen were so miserably reduced as to be incapable " of extricating themselves from that slavery forged for them by the corrupt influence of the Crown ";

[1] *L. P.*, Aug. 11, 1773.

but, on the other side of the Atlantic, " Our brave American fellow-subjects are not yet corrupted, but gloriously stand up in defence of their undoubted rights and liberties; and whilst they shall maintain them by their public virtue and fortitude, they will defend the freedom of their aged parent country from all the infirmities, evils, and oppression of time, corruption and arbitrary power." [1]

Many Englishmen considered the cause of America a common cause and there is evidence that some colonists considered the cause of liberty in England, as championed by Wilkes, to be common to them, for on Wilkes's birthday in 1769, among other presents given to him by Americans were forty-five hogsheads of tobacco.[2]   Shortly afterwards the gift of £1500 by the Assembly of South Carolina, to the Supporters of the Bill of Rights Society was reported.[3] This society defended Wilkes as a supporter of the English constitution.   In a letter of thanks to South Carolina, the Supporters of the Bill of Rights stated, " Our cause is one—our enemies are the same." Continuing, they desired that the Americans would remain firm in their resistance to tyranny, for such action confirmed their hopes that " when luxury, misrule, and corruption shall at length, in spite of all resistance, have destroyed this noble Constitution here, our posterity will not, like your gallant ancestors, be driven to an inhospitable shore, but will find a welcome refuge, . . . amongst their fellow subjects, the descendants and brothers of Englishmen." [4]

[1] *K. G.*, Jan. 7, 1775; see *L. C.*, Oct. 12, 1769; *L. P.*, July 27, 1774.

[2] *Gent. Mag.*, October, 1769, p. 509.

[3] *Gent. Mag.*, Feb., 1770, p. 94; *P. A.*, Feb. 7, 1770; see " John Wilkes and Boston," *Mass. Hist. Soc. Procs.*, vol. 47, pp. 190-214; see Bleackley, *Life of Wilkes*, p. 243 *et seq.*

[4] *Gent. Mag.*, July, 1770, p. 312; *Univ. Mag. Supp.*, 1770; see *Middlesex Journal or Chronicle of Liberty*, June 15, 1771; *P. A.* for the same period.

Englishmen were urged to champion America, for, in the words of "The Colonist's Advocate," "should an encroaching Adminstration prevail in enslaving the Colonies, would they not thence be emboldened to subject the Mother-Country to their Iron Rod?"[1] "Serious Truth" maintained "that the Cause of Liberty in England and in America" was "ONE COMMON CAUSE." The attacks on both had been made "and carried on by the same Set of Men, with the same Views, and with the same illegal Violence."[2] A reading of the papers leaves no doubt of the strength and sincerity of this argument.[3]

An analysis of sentiment among English social classes reveals that the landed interest was consistently for strong measures against the Americans. Reference has been made to this before,[4] but it came out most clearly in 1775. The advocates of a strong American policy urged that all depended upon the representatives of the landed gentry. These same advocates were charged with attempting to set the land owners against the traders and manufacturers. The landed interest was warned to beware lest in alienating America the harm redound upon their own heads.[5] It was stated that Lord North had often plumed himself on their support, and that they had been bribed to enter the lists against America "by a Shilling in the Pound Land Tax."[6] The evidence is clear that this group, which was probably the most influential political group in England, was against the Americans.

[1] *P. A.*, Jan. 29, 1770.

[2] *S. J. C.*, Feb. 14, 1769.

[3] For this point of view see *Univ. Mag.*, July, 1770, p. 51, Supp. for 1774, p. 364; *K. G.*, June 11, Dec. 24, 1774; *L. P.*, Nov. 11, 1774, Dec. 21, 1774; *L. C.*, Feb. 11, 1775; *London Mag.*, Jan., 1766 *passim*.

[4] *Supra*, Townshend Acts, notes 2, 3. Stamp Act, notes 4, 5, 6.

[5] See *P. A.*, Jan. 26, Feb. 2, 1775; *L. C.*, Jan. 31, March 2, 1775; *S. J. C.*, Feb. 4, 1775; *L. P.*, April 12, Feb. 17, Aug. 2, 1775.

[6] *S. J. C.*, June 10, 1775; see *K. G.*, July 29, Nov. 18, 1775.

On the other hand the evidence examined just as clearly shows that the great merchants were almost always friendly to the American cause. The manufacturers also favored reconciliation with the Americans, but their views were not quite so pronounced as those of the traders.

This division of class interests may be a help in understanding why the pro-American advocates were so well represented in the papers. Provincial journalism, as we have seen, had little individuality of its own. Over all England it was largely a reflection of the press of London, and hence it was little likely to be representative of the land-owning group. The printers, by every canon of class interest, were allied to the merchants, not to the landed aristocracy. Socially and economically they belonged to the rising middle class. When to this is added the fact that the press was very frequently persecuted by the members of the dominant group, the appearance of so much opinion in opposition to the government is more understandable.

When we consider the ecclesiastical party in England we find the landed interest again. The Church of England was identified with the land-owning aristocracy. Their interests were the same and their policy was the same. Only two members of the episcopal bench took a pro-American stand. They were Jonathan Shipley, Bishop of St. Asaph, a close friend to Benjamin Franklin, and Hinchliffe, Bishop of Peterborough.[1] The former on February 19, 1773, preached a strongly pro-American sermon before the Society for the Propagation of the Gospel, which was widely quoted and warmly approved by the friends of the American cause.[2] The attitude of the Church of England was well displayed also in the bishop controversy. The church was clearly against the Americans.[3]

[1] See article on Jonathan Shipley in *D. N. B.*
[2] *S. J. C.,* June 30, 1774; see *M. J. & E. A.,* Dec. 20, 1774.
[3] See *L. C.,* Sept. 16, 1775.

Opposed to the church by natural alignment was the non-conformist interest.   That, too, was evidenced in the bishop controversy.   Their attitude may have been prompted by a fellow feeling for their non-conformist brethren in America, by their Puritan inheritance which set them against the established church, and by the very natural tendency to oppose a group over them that was often domineering and always aristocratic.   The attitude the Quakers displayed in 1775 shows them joined with the opponents of strong action against the colonists.

All the groups in England which were of the opposition would naturally tend to take a pro-American attitude as a matter of political strategy.

To try to estimate the weight of public opinion at any time is a task of the greatest hazard, and is not here attempted. To do so in the period under review would be especially difficult.   Many have endeavored to weigh it by studying the acts of the public men of the day.   " Pacificus " pointed out some of the dangers of such a proceeding.   He observed, " From the great Majority (observable in certain Places) of Persons, who are for violent Measures with the Americans, some may, perhaps, be ready to conclude, that those Measures are in the same Proportion agreeable to the People of this Country."   But he thought such a method would not be allowed a sure one, especially in the present case :

if we consider how much the far greater Part of our leading Men (as I shall call them) are evidently influenced in their Judgements and Determinations, not by Arguments of Reason, Dictates of Justice or Humanity, or a regard to the Public Good; but by other and less honourable Considerations; which, though they may influence some of the common People, can be supposed to influence but few of them in Comparison. . . . This . . . is abundantly sufficient to show that there is no judging with Certainty of the Sentiments of the People, from the professed Sentiments of our Great Men. . . . [1]

It is evident, therefore, that the friends of America in England were not limited to a few advocates in Parliament but included a large and very vocal group outside, and that the War of the American Revolution was in a very real sense a civil war.

[1] *S. J. C.*, June 8, 1775.

APPENDIX

In almost all cases the attempts to identify pseudonyms have been unsuccessful. The following identifications, however, have been made:

"Anti-Sejanus." The Reverend James Scott.

"Amor Patriae." Thomas Crowley. Crowley also used many other newspaper signatures, but the letters signed thus are the only ones used in this study. See *Dissertations on the grand dispute between Great Britain and America* (1774), *Letters and Dissertations on various subjects*, and *Copies of Letters and Dissertations since March 7, 1773*.

"Britannicus." Allan Ramsay Jr. See *Letters on the present disturbances in Great Britain and her American Provinces* (London, 1777).

"Cassandra." Josiah Tucker. See *Dictionary of National Biography*.

"Columbus." No certain identification but a *London Evening Post* contributor of Jan. 21, 1775, called him "Columbus" Shebbeare. See Shebbeare in *Dictionary of National Biography*.

"Constitutio." Major John Cartwright.

"Constitution." According to Cushing, *Initials and Pseudonyms*, also Major Cartwright.

"Curtius." Probably Dr. William Jackson.

"Numa." No certain identification but the *London Evening Post* writer above referred to, on Jan. 21, 1775, called him "Numa" Kelly, probably in reference to William Kelly, the New York merchant, who was in London at the time.

"Old Slyboots." Another name used by the Reverend James Scott.

"Sylvanus Urban." Used by the editor of the *Gentleman's Magazine*.

LONDON NEWSPAPERS AND MAGAZINES

Bingley's Journal or the Universal Gazette.
The Critical Review: or, Annals of Literature.
The Daily Advertiser.
The Gazetteer and New Daily Advertiser.
The General Evening Post.
The Gentleman's Magazine, and Historical Chronicle.
Lloyd's Evening Post, and British Chronicle.
The London Chronicle.
The London Evening Post.
The London Gazette.

The London Magazine.
The London Packet.
The Middlesex Journal or Chronicle of Liberty.
The Middlesex Journal and Evening Advertiser.
The Middlesex Journal or Universal Evening Post. A continuation of
   M. J. or C. L.
The Morning Chronicle, and London Advertiser.
The Morning Post, and Daily Advertiser.
The Monthly Review.
The Public Ledger.
The St. James's Chronicle; or the British Evening Post.
The Town and Country Magazine.
The Universal Magazine, of Knowledge and Pleasure.
The Whisperer.
The Whitehall Evening-Post: or, London Intelligencer.

PROVINCIAL PAPERS

Adam's Weekly Courant (Chester).
The British Chronicle, or Pugh's Hereford Journal.
The Chelmsford and Colchester Chronicle: or Universal Weekly Advertiser (Chelmsford).
The Chester Chronicle; or, Commercial Intelligencer.
The Gloucester Journal.
The Ipswich Journal.
Jackson's Oxford Journal.
The Kentish Gazette (Canterbury).
The Newcastle Chronicle, or *Weekly Advertiser, and Register of News, Commerce & Entertainment.*
The Newcastle Journal.
The Northampton Mercury.
The Norwich Mercury.

PAMPHLETS AND CONTEMPORARY SOURCES

Cartwright, John. *American Independence; the Interest and Glory of Great Britain* (London, 1774). This was originally a series of newspaper letters.
Crowley, Thomas. *Copies of Letters and Dissertations since March 7, 1773.*
Crowley, Thomas. *Letters and Dissertations on Various Subjects* (London, probably 1776).
de Berdt, Dennys. *Letters of Dennys de Berdt, 1757-1770,* Colon. Soc. Mass. Pubs., vol. xiii, pp. 293-461.
Eddis, W. *Letters from America, 1769-1777* (London, 1792).
Force, Peter. *American Archives.* 4th Series (1837-53, Washington).

Franklin, Benjamin. *The Writings of Benjamin Franklin.* Albert H. Smyth, editor. 10 vols. (New York, 1907).

Lee, Arthur. *The Political Detection; or, the Treachery and Tyranny of Administration, Both at Home and Abroad; Displayed in a Series of Letters Signed Junius Americanus* (London, 1770).

Lee, Richard Henry. *Letters.* 2 vols. (J. C. Ballagh, ed., New York, 1912).

Maseres, Francis. *Occasional Letters on Various Subjects* (London, 1809).

Nichols, John. *Literary Anecdotes of the Eighteenth Century.* Six vols. (London, 1812).

Pownall, Thomas. *Administration of the Colonies* (London, 1764). This subsequently went through many editions and was very much enlarged. See Pownall, C. A. W., *Thomas Pownall.*

Ramsay, Allan Jr. *Letters on the Present Disturbances in Great Britain and Her American Provinces* (London, 1777).

Tucker, Josiah. *The Respective Pleas and Arguments of the Mother Country, and of the Colonies distinctly set forth, and the Impossibility of a Compromise of Differences, or a mutual Concession of Rights plainly demonstrated* (1774).

Wilkes, John. *John Wilkes and Boston.* Mass. His. Soc. Procs., vol. 47, pp. 190-214.

BOOKS ON NEWSPAPERS

Andrews, Alexander. *History of British Journalism.* 2 vols. (London, 1859).

Athenaeum. July 29, 1848.

Austin, Roland. *Robert Raikes, the Elder, and the Gloucester Journal* (London, 1915).

Bourne, H. R. Fox. *English Newspapers.* 2 vols. (London, 1887).

Cambridge History of English Literature (Cambridge, 1907-1916).

Grant, James. *The Newspaper Press: its origin, progress and present position.* 3 vols. (London, 1871).

Hunt, Frederick Knight. *The Fourth Estate: Contributions towards a History of the Liberty of the Press* (London, 1850).

Macdonagh, Michael. *The Reporter's Gallery* (London, 1913).

May, Thomas Erskine. *The Constitutional History of England Since the Accession of George the Third.* 3 vols. (London, 1912). Vol. ii, chap. ix.

History of the Northampton Mercury (Northampton, England, 1901).

Pebody, Charles. *English Journalism and the Men who have Made It* (London, 1882).

Porritt, Edward and Annie G. *The Unreformed House of Commons.* 2 vols. (Cambridge, 1903). Vol. i, chap. xxx.

Salmon, L. M. *The Newspaper and the Historian* (New York, 1923).
Tercentenary Handlist of English & Welsh Newspapers, Magazines & Reviews (London: The Times, 1920).
Timperley, C. H. *A Dictionary of Printers and Printing* (London, 1838).
Williams, J. B. *History of English Journalism* (London, New York, 1908).

GENERAL SECONDARY AUTHORITIES

Adams, Randolph Greenfield. *Political Ideas of the American Revolution* (Trinity College Press, 1922).
Alvord, Clarence Walworth. *Mississippi Valley in British Politics.* 2 vols. (Cleveland, 1917).
Andrews, C. M. *The Colonial Background of the American Revolution* (New Haven, 1924).
Beer, G. L. *British Colonial Policy, 1754-1765* (New York, 1907).
Beer, G. L. *The Commercial Policy of England toward the American Colonies* (Col. Univ. Studies, vol. iii, no. 2), (New York, 1893).
Berry, William. *History of the Island of Guernsey* (London, 1815).
Bleackley, Horace. *Life of John Wilkes* (London, 1917).
Channing, Edward. *A History of the United States.* Vol. iii, (New York, 1912).
Cross, Arthur Lyon. *The Anglican Episcopate and the American Colonies* (Harvard Historical Studies, 1902).
Cushing, William. *Anonyms.* 2 vols. (London, 1890).
Cushing, William. *Initials and Pseudonyms: A Dictionary of Literary Disguises* (New York, 1885).
Dictionary of National Biography (London, 1899).
Fisher, Sydney George. *The Struggle for American Independence.* 2 vols. (London, 1908).
Frey, Albert R. *Soubriquets and Nicknames* (London, 1887).
Frothingham, R. *The Rise of the Republic of the United States* (Boston, 1881).
Haines, Charles Grove. *The American Doctrine of Judicial Supremacy* (New York, 1914).
Halkett, Samuel and Laing, John. *A Dictionary of the Anonymous and Pseudonymous Literature of Great Britain.* 4 vols. (Edinburgh, 1882).
Howard, George Elliott. *Preliminaries of the American Revolution* (American Nation Series), (New York and London, 1905).
Kingsford, William. *The History of Canada.* 10 vols. (London, 1892).
Lecky, W. E. H. *History of England in the Eighteenth Century.* 8 vols. (London, 1878-1909).
Lee, R. H. *Life of Arthur Lee.* 2 vols. (Boston, 1829).

MacDonald, William. *Select Charters and Other Documents Illustrative of American History*, 1606-1775 (New York, 1899).

MacNevin, Thomas. *The Lives and Trials of Archibald Hamilton Rowan, The Rev. William Jackson etc.* (Dublin, 1846).

Marks, Mary A. M. *England and America 1763-1783.* 2 vols. (London, 1907).

McIlwain, Charles Howard. *The American Revolution: A Constitutional Interpretation* (New York, 1923).

McIlwain, Charles Howard. *The High Court of Parliament and Its Supremacy* (New Haven, 1910).

McLaughlin, Andrew Cunningham. *America and Britain* (New York, 1918).

McLaughlin, Andrew Cunningham. *The Courts, The Constitution and Parties* (Chicago, 1912).

Miller, Samuel. *A Brief Retrospect of the Eighteenth Century.* 3 vols. (London, 1805).

Pownall, Charles A. W. *Thomas Pownall* (London, 1908).

Schlesinger, Arthur Meier. *The Colonial Merchants and the American Revolution, 1763-1776* (Columbia Univ. Studies, vol. lxviii), (New York, 1917).

Sharpless, Isaac. *The Quakers in the Revolution* (Philadelphia, 1899).

Trevelyan, G. O. *The American Revolution.* 4 vols. (New York, 1899-1912).

Tyler, Moses Coit. *The Literary History of the American Revolution, 1763-178?.* 2 vols. (New York, 1897).

Van Tyne, C. H. *Causes of the War of Independence* (Boston, 1922).

INDEX

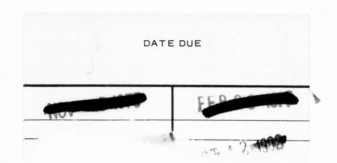